STUFF YOU SHOULD KNOW ABOUT PLANET EARTH

Quarto is the authority on a wide range of topics.
Quarto educates, entertains and enriches the lives of
our readers—enthusiasts and lovers of hands-on living.
www.quartoknows.com

This edition first published in 2018
by QED Publishing,
an imprint of The Quarto Group.
The Old Brewery, 6 Blundell Street,
London N7 9BH, United Kingdom.
T (0)20 7700 6700 F (0)20 7700 8066
www.QuartoKnows.com

A catalogue record for this book is available
from the British Library.

Author: John Farndon
Illustrator: Tim Hutchinson
Editorial Director: Laura Knowles
Art Director: Susi Martin
Creative Director: Malena Stojic
Publisher: Maxime Boucknooghe
Designed and edited by Tall Tree Ltd

ISBN 978-1-912413-66-9

Manufactured in Dongguan, China TL072018

9 8 7 6 5 4 3 2 1

STUFF YOU SHOULD KNOW ABOUT
PLANET EARTH

John Farndon

Tim Hutchinson

QED

CONTENTS

* INDICATES A GATEFOLD SECTION

WELCOME TO THE WORLD!

Earth is very old – 5.43 billion years old, in fact. But it's also a fantastical realm of spouting volcanoes, surging rivers, whirling storms, forests teeming with life... and that's just the start. Come and join our band of little people as they reveal some of its secrets! On our journey, we will visit the Earth's five amazing, interwoven 'spheres'.

SOLID EARTH

We could wander over the geosphere – the solid Earth. This is Earth's rocks and stones, its mountains and its continents, and its hot interior. They are all made from a marvellous mix of materials: 32% iron, 30% oxygen, 15% silicon, 14% magnesium, 3% sulphur, 2% nickel as well as calcium, aluminium and various trace elements.

GEOSPHERE

HYDROSPHERE

WATER WORLD

Why not plunge into the hydrosphere? The glistening world of water consists of Earth's rivers, lakes, streams, oceans, groundwater, polar ice caps, glaciers and moisture in the air (like rain and snow). It's mostly on the surface, but also seeps several kilometres down, as well as up into the atmosphere. It makes Earth very special.

THE ICE REALM

Perhaps you'd like to shiver in the cryosphere? This glittering ice realm is where water freezes solid. It's in ice sheets on land in Greenland and Antarctica, as well as in ice caps, glaciers, snow and permafrost. It's also on water in the frozen ocean around Antarctica and the Arctic and frozen rivers and lakes, which mainly occur in polar areas.

THE KINGDOMS OF LIFE

Then there's the most miraculous realm of all, the biosphere. This is the living world and contains all the animals, plants and microbes that swim, fly, crawl, run, or just live in almost every nook on Earth. More than 1.25 million species of animal have been identified, and there are likely to be many more. Earth is the only place we know that has life.

CRYOSPHERE

BIOSPHERE

ATMOSPHERE

AIR BLANKET

Maybe we can float up into the atmosphere? Earth's invisible envelope of air stretches more than 10,000 km up from the surface, before trailing away into space. It is a heady mix of nitrogen (about 78%), oxygen (about 21%) and other gases (about 1%), such as carbon dioxide (0.039%), argon (0.93%) and trace gases (krypton, neon, helium and xenon).

7

HOW DOES THE EARTH MOVE?

THE SUNWHIRLER

Our world is a tiny, bright ball, spinning in the vastness of space. But it's not alone – it's part of a family of worlds gathered round the Sun. Our family is called the solar system and we all whirl through space together, as if on a giant carousel.

1. SCORCHING HEART

The Sun really is huge. You could fit the Earth inside it 1.3 million times! The Sun's mass exerts such a strong pull that the rest of the solar system is forced to spin around it.

2. THE GIANT FAMILY

Seven other big, round worlds or 'planets' enjoy the carousel ride with Earth, and hundreds of balls called moons circle these planets. In between are millions of rocky asteroids – and icy comets that whizz in and out.

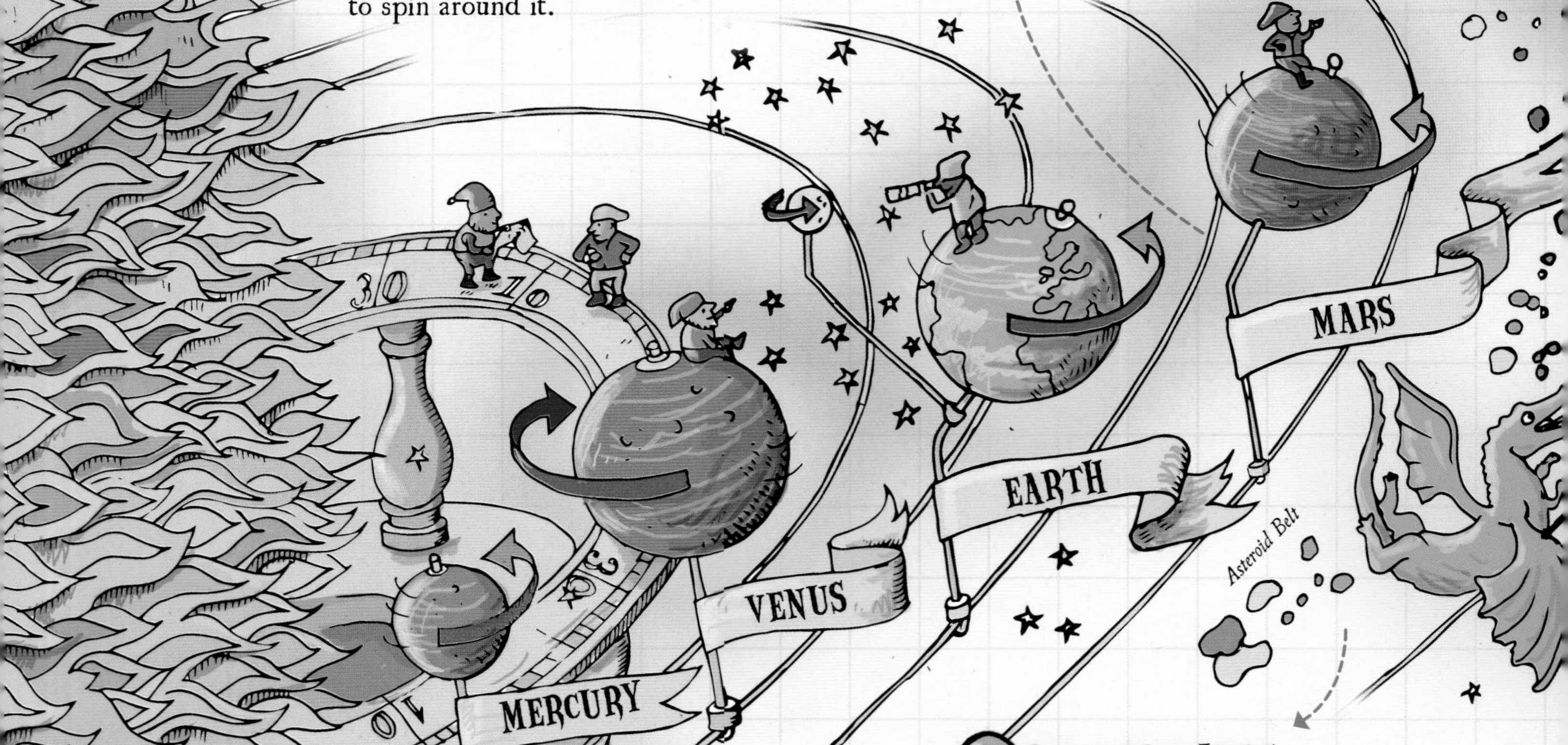

MARS

EARTH

VENUS

Asteroid Belt

MERCURY

3. ROCK BROTHERS

The four inner planets that circle close to the Sun – Mercury, Venus, Earth and Mars – are made mostly of rock. Out beyond Mars is a band of asteroids called the Asteroid Belt.

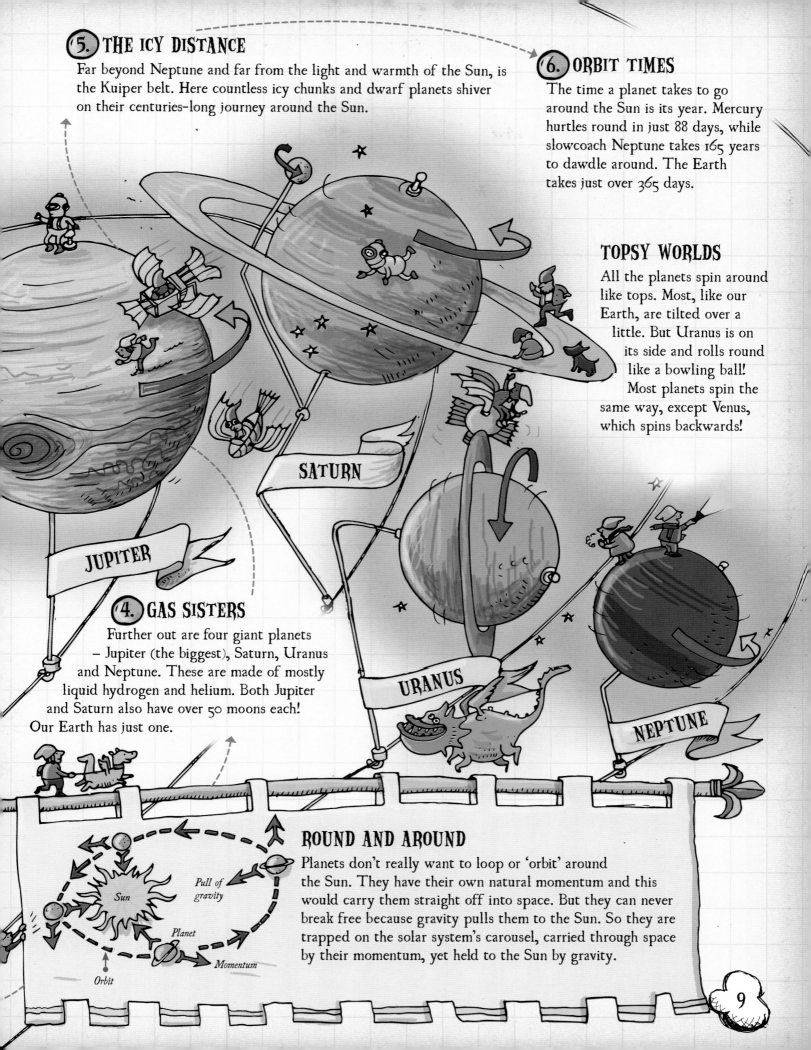

5. THE ICY DISTANCE

Far beyond Neptune and far from the light and warmth of the Sun, is the Kuiper belt. Here countless icy chunks and dwarf planets shiver on their centuries-long journey around the Sun.

6. ORBIT TIMES

The time a planet takes to go around the Sun is its year. Mercury hurtles round in just 88 days, while slowcoach Neptune takes 165 years to dawdle around. The Earth takes just over 365 days.

TOPSY WORLDS

All the planets spin around like tops. Most, like our Earth, are tilted over a little. But Uranus is on its side and rolls round like a bowling ball! Most planets spin the same way, except Venus, which spins backwards!

SATURN

JUPITER

4. GAS SISTERS

Further out are four giant planets – Jupiter (the biggest), Saturn, Uranus and Neptune. These are made of mostly liquid hydrogen and helium. Both Jupiter and Saturn also have over 50 moons each! Our Earth has just one.

URANUS

NEPTUNE

ROUND AND AROUND

Pull of gravity

Sun

Planet

Orbit

Momentum

Planets don't really want to loop or 'orbit' around the Sun. They have their own natural momentum and this would carry them straight off into space. But they can never break free because gravity pulls them to the Sun. So they are trapped on the solar system's carousel, carried through space by their momentum, yet held to the Sun by gravity.

WHY DO WE HAVE NIGHT AND DAY?

WHO'S MOVING?
To us on Earth, it looks as if the Sun is moving across the sky. But in fact it's the Earth spinning round, while the Sun stays in the same place all the time.

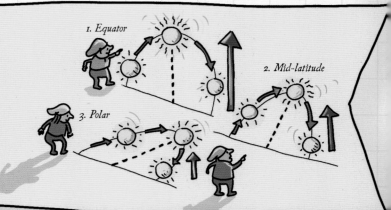

Night

Sunlight

Day

The Earth might seem still, but it's whizzing round at 1,600 km/h right now! Every 24 hours it spins all the way round to face the Sun and then away again, giving us night and day.

North Pole

Sun

1. GOLDEN DAWN

Earth always spins the same way, from west to east. Every day, wherever you are, your part of Earth turns east to face the Sun. The Sun seems to burst above the horizon, casting long shadows, and day begins.

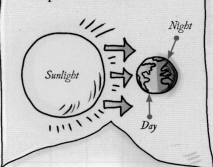

2. MORNING SUN

As Earth spins on eastwards, the Sun seems to climb in the sky. It's soon well above the horizon and shining brightly, casting strong shadows across the landscape.

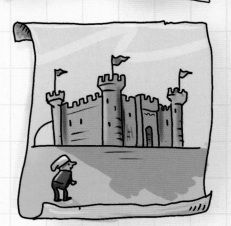

HIGH AND LOW SUN

1. The nearer you get to the Equator, the higher the Sun climbs in the sky and the more strongly it shines. That's why it's warm here. **2.** Because of the curve of the Earth, the Sun climbs less high away from the Equator, making it cooler, and shadows longer. **3.** At the poles, the Sun is very low in the sky. In winter, it doesn't even rise above the horizon.

1. Equator

2. Mid-latitude

3. Polar

10

3. BRIGHT NOON

By midday or 'noon', we are turned to face the Sun directly. The Sun is at its highest point in the sky, called the zenith. It's at its brightest and shadows are short. In summer, this is when the day starts getting really hot!

4. GOOD AFTERNOON

After noon, the Sun begins to sink, as Earth spins you away again, and the shadows get longer. It is often the hottest time of day, because the air has been warmed all day.

5. SUNDOWN

As Earth spins on, the Sun begins to sink below the horizon. At sunset, it shines at a slant through the air and its light is scattered by dust and water vapour, often turning the sky red. With the Sun so low, shadows are very long.

6. DARK NIGHT

Finally, the Sun disappears beyond the horizon and night begins. The sky is dark, and we can now see the distant stars, invisible during the day because the sky was so bright. From space, you can see twinkling lights of cities.

WHY DOES THE MOON CHANGE SHAPE?

If you watch the Moon for a month, it seems to change shape, starting as a crescent, then growing to a ball, then back to a crescent again. But the Moon's changing shape, known as its 'phases', are all a trick of the light!

1. THE DARK SIDE

As it orbits Earth, the Moon turns so slowly that it keeps the same side facing us all the time. This is what you see in the sky. What you can't see is the far side because it stays pointing away from us all the time.

2. SHAPE SHIFTER

As the Moon travels round Earth, it seems to change shape each night. Really, all that is happening is that we are getting different views of the bright side from Earth.

Waxing gibbous

Full Moon

Waning gibbous

SILVERY MOON

The Moon is the biggest, brightest thing in the night sky. But it has no light of its own – it is just a cold ball of rock. It shines because it reflects the light from the Sun.

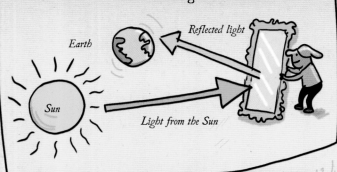

Earth

Reflected light

Sun

Light from the Sun

3. FULL MOON

The Moon takes just less than a month to go round the Earth, so the phases go through a monthly cycle. When the Moon is on the far side of the Earth from the Sun, all its bright side is visible. You see a full disc, called the Full Moon.

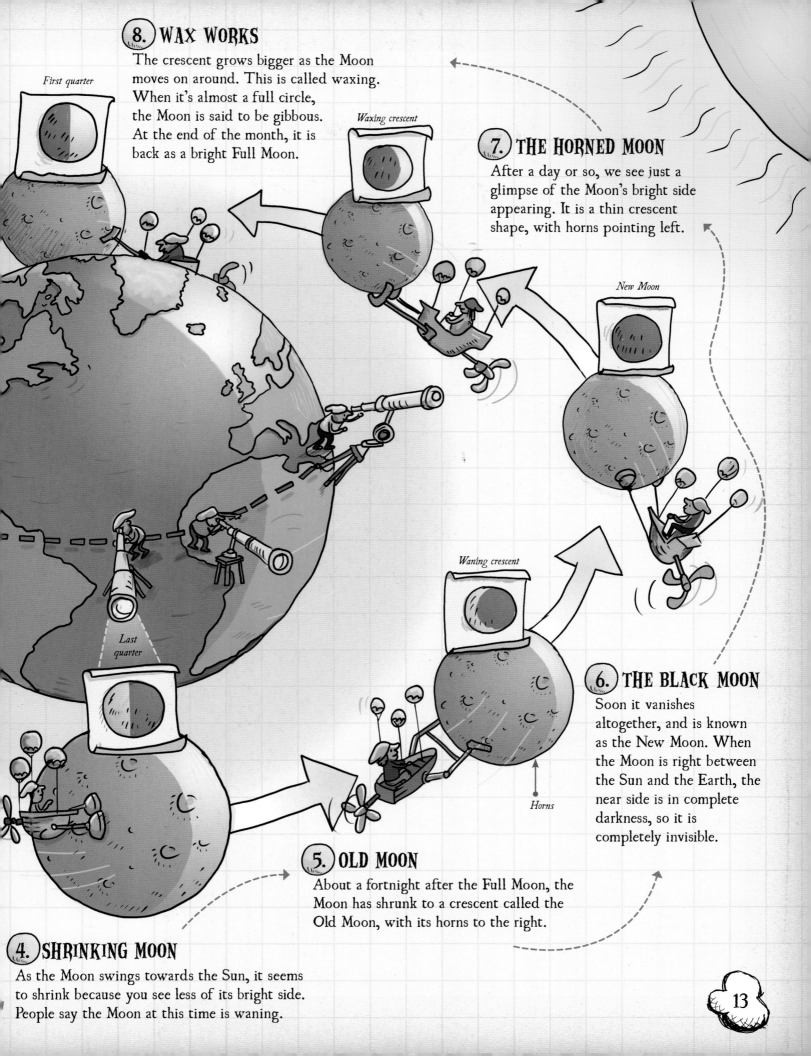

8. WAX WORKS

The crescent grows bigger as the Moon moves on around. This is called waxing. When it's almost a full circle, the Moon is said to be gibbous. At the end of the month, it is back as a bright Full Moon.

First quarter

Waxing crescent

7. THE HORNED MOON

After a day or so, we see just a glimpse of the Moon's bright side appearing. It is a thin crescent shape, with horns pointing left.

New Moon

Last quarter

Waning crescent

Horns

6. THE BLACK MOON

Soon it vanishes altogether, and is known as the New Moon. When the Moon is right between the Sun and the Earth, the near side is in complete darkness, so it is completely invisible.

5. OLD MOON

About a fortnight after the Full Moon, the Moon has shrunk to a crescent called the Old Moon, with its horns to the right.

4. SHRINKING MOON

As the Moon swings towards the Sun, it seems to shrink because you see less of its bright side. People say the Moon at this time is waning.

WHAT'S INSIDE THE EARTH?

You may think you're standing on solid ground, but beneath your feet, Earth plunges some 6,371 km down to its core, and on the way it gets hot and complicated.

LITHOSPHERE

ASTHENOSPHERE

MANTLE

Melting lithosphere

Crust

Moho

Mantle plume

1. CRUSTY

What you're standing on is just a thin rocky crust floating on top, like the skin on custard. Under the continents, there are ancient chunks of crust 70 km thick, but the crust under the oceans is much newer and thinner.

2. MOHO HO

If you could drill down through the crust, you'd reach the Moho – where the crust ends and Earth's 'mantle' begins. The mantle is made of superdense rock, much denser than the crust. It's nearly 3,000 km deep and superhot – reaching over 3,000°C near the bottom!

3. THE STIFF BIT

The top of the mantle is rigid and stuck to the underside of the crust. Geologists call this sandwich of the crust and upper mantle the lithosphere.

4. HOT AND TREACLY

Earth gets hotter as you go deeper. About 100 km down, it reaches a scorching 1,280°C – hot enough to melt rock! Here the lithosphere melts into the treacly asthenosphere. The melted rock is called magma.

Boundary

5. CRACKING UP

In some places in the world, slabs of lithosphere slide into cracks. They are pulled down thousands of kilometres into the hot mantle, melting as they go – until they finally disintegrate.

7. FIRE FOUNTAINS

Wrapped around the CMB is a stormy ocean of hot rock 100 km deep called the D" (D double prime). As it churns about, this spouts fiery fountains of hot rock called mantle plumes that shoot up and up to Earth's surface.

6. CLANG!!!

Just under 3,000 km down, with temperatures soaring over 3,000°C, you suddenly strike metal. This is the Core–Mantle Boundary (CMB). Beneath lies Earth's superdense, superhot core of iron and nickel.

8. CORE!

The inner core is as hot as the surface of the Sun, over 6,000°C. With all that rock and iron above it, though, the pressure here is so extreme that the metal simply cannot melt. Instead, it's superdense crystalline metal.

OUTER CORE

INNER CORE

D" (double prime)

THE METAL DYNAMO

The outer core is so hot, the metal here is melted to liquid. As Earth spins through space, this metal swirls around. It becomes a giant dynamo, creating magnetic currents that turn the whole Earth into a mighty magnet.

15

HOW DO THE CONTINENTS MOVE?

You might think the world has always been the same, but the continents actually drift around very slowly, pushed and pulled by currents in the mantle below. Over long periods, they have come together and broken apart many times, like a huge jigsaw.

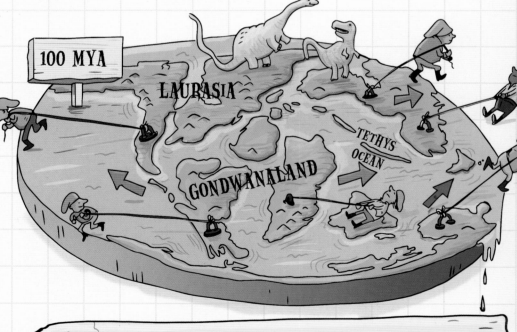

200 MYA

1. GIANT PANGEA

Long ago, before even dinosaurs began to stomp around, all the world's continents were joined together in one giant land mass. Today, scientists call this supercontinent 'Pangea'.

2. THE WIDEST OCEAN

Surrounding Pangea was a single vast ocean. Scientists now call it Panthalassa. It covered two thirds of the Earth. If you sailed out from the western shore of Pangea, you could journey 30,000 km, until you reached land again on the eastern shore of Pangea!

3. THE GIANT CRACKS

About 200 million years ago (mya), Pangea began to tear apart. Volcanoes burst through from beneath, and large slabs of it pulled apart. It split almost in half to create two new continents, Laurasia in the north and Gondwanaland in the south.

100 MYA

LAURASIA

GONDWANALAND

TETHYS OCEAN

DINO DAYS

Dinosaurs appeared 235 million years ago, when Pangea was at its biggest. For 170 million years as Pangea broke up, dinosaurs were the kings of the world. Then 66 million years ago, they mysteriously vanished.

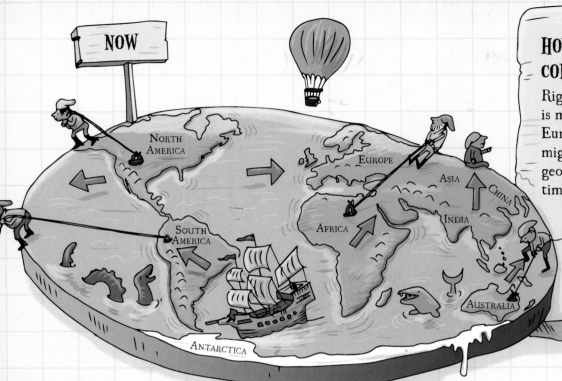

NOW

NORTH AMERICA

EUROPE

ASIA

CHINA

INDIA

AFRICA

SOUTH AMERICA

AUSTRALIA

ANTARCTICA

HOW FAST DO CONTINENTS MOVE?

Right now, North America is moving 2.5 cm away from Europe every year. That might not sound much, but geology has lots and lots of time. In a million years, America moves 25 km. In 100 million years, it can move 2500 km, though some continents move even faster!

7. THE WORLD TODAY

Continents are still moving, even today. North America is shifting slowly further from Europe. Africa is rotating clockwise, splitting in the northeast, but also squeezing the Mediterranean Sea against Europe. Australia, meanwhile, is powering north towards China.

6. THE ATLANTIC IS BORN

By 50 mya, the dinosaurs were gone. In the north, a new ocean, the Atlantic, opened between America and Europe. In the south, India had broken away from Africa and was heading north to smash into Asia.

50 MYA

NORTH AMERICA

ATLANTIC OCEAN

EUROPE

ASIA

AFRICA

INDIA

SOUTH AMERICA

AUSTRALIA

ANTARCTICA

5. THE AGE OF ISLANDS

By 100 mya, the landmasses were entirely broken into the fragments that would become today's continents. But the continents were swamped and the oceans were dotted with thousands and thousands of tiny tropical islands – more islands than ever. Europe was just a sea of islands.

4. A NEW SEA

In between Laurasia and Gondwanaland, right along the Equator, a new sea, the Tethys Ocean, sparkled and splashed in the tropical sun. Just as the dinosaurs ruled the land, so giant reptiles, such as plesiosaurs, ruled these seas.

17

5. ASH FALL
Destroyed fragments of the plug rise up in a vast cloud of ash and cinder, then fall like rain far around, covering the ground in a thick, hot, choking blanket.

Ash and cinder cloud

Falling ash

4. GAS AND WATER BLAST
Now the volcano explodes. Scalding jets of steam and vast clouds of ash and cinder shoot high in the air. Then magma gushes out the top and turns into red-hot lava that streams down the sides of the volcano.

3. BLAST OFF
Soon, the rising magma pushes the plug right out, and the pressure in the magma is suddenly released – it's like the top coming off a fizzy-drink bottle. Carbon dioxide and water in the magma fizzes into bubbles and powers the magma up the vent.

Plug

Vent

Magma chamber

2. VOLCANIC STOPPER
A chimney or vent leads up from the chamber to the top of the cone of debris built up by previous eruptions. Often, a plug of magma solidifies in the vent, blocking it up like the cork in a bottle.

WHAT MAKES VOLCANOES ERUPT?

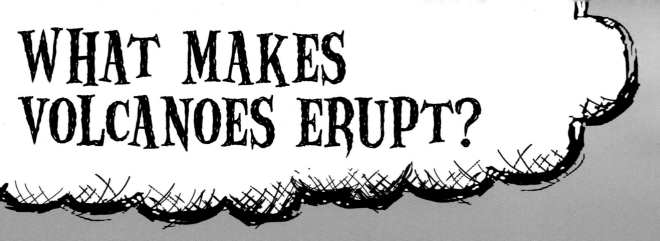

Volcanoes are leaks in the Earth's crust – places where red-hot liquid rock (magma) from underground bursts onto the surface. Sometimes, the magma oozes out slowly. But other times it explodes with a rumble and a mighty roar, blasting out ash and fiery gases and streams of lava.

THE VOLCANO MAP

About 500 volcanoes around the world could erupt any second! Most lie along the cracks between tectonic plates. There are lots around the edge of the Pacific Ocean, giving it a 'Ring of Fire'.

1. THE VOLCANO'S OVEN

Deep under some kinds of volcano, there's a vast cavern called a magma chamber. Before an eruption, it fills with magma (molten rock) that wells up from Earth's hot interior.

Ring of Fire

HOW IS THE CRUST CRACKED?

Even as you read this book, the land under your feet is moving. All Earth's surface is cracked into giant slabs of rock called tectonic plates. So continents are very slowly splitting apart or crunching together, while new oceans are opening up or being crushed into nothing.

1. PIECES OF THE EARTH

Tectonic plates are the cracked pieces of the world's stiff outer shell or lithosphere. There are seven gigantic plates, ten smaller plates and dozens of 'micro' plates.

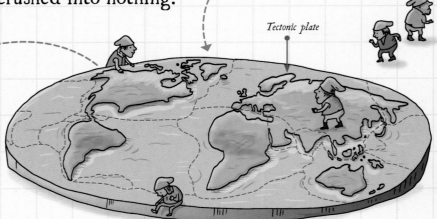

Tectonic plate

2. OCEANS AND CONTINENTS

The biggest plate is the Pacific Plate. It spreads all the way under the Pacific Ocean and is almost entirely underwater. All the other plates carry continents. The continents are made of light, very ancient rock and ride on the plates.

3. SLIPPING AND SLIDING

In some places, called transforms, the plates are neither crashing together nor pulling apart. Instead, they are sliding past each other in opposite directions. As the edges scrape and grind past each other they set off violent earthquakes.

4. STRETCH!

In other places, the crack between the plates is being yanked apart. When this happens under the oceans, hot melted rock from Earth's interior oozes up and cools to form a giant ridge on the sea bed. If it happens on land, a deep valley called a rift opens up.

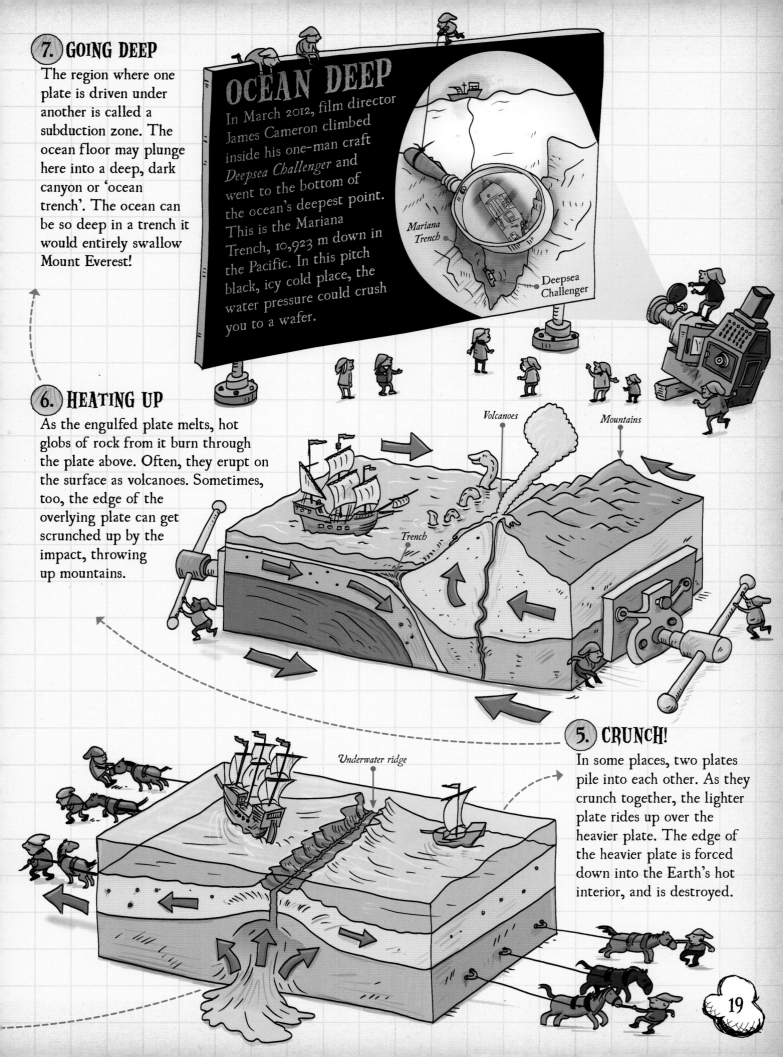

7. GOING DEEP

The region where one plate is driven under another is called a subduction zone. The ocean floor may plunge here into a deep, dark canyon or 'ocean trench'. The ocean can be so deep in a trench it would entirely swallow Mount Everest!

OCEAN DEEP

In March 2012, film director James Cameron climbed inside his one-man craft *Deepsea Challenger* and went to the bottom of the ocean's deepest point. This is the Mariana Trench, 10,923 m down in the Pacific. In this pitch black, icy cold place, the water pressure could crush you to a wafer.

Mariana Trench

Deepsea Challenger

6. HEATING UP

As the engulfed plate melts, hot globs of rock from it burn through the plate above. Often, they erupt on the surface as volcanoes. Sometimes, too, the edge of the overlying plate can get scrunched up by the impact, throwing up mountains.

Volcanoes

Mountains

Trench

5. CRUNCH!

In some places, two plates pile into each other. As they crunch together, the lighter plate rides up over the heavier plate. The edge of the heavier plate is forced down into the Earth's hot interior, and is destroyed.

Underwater ridge

19

VOLCANO GALLERY

Volcanoes come in different sizes and shapes.

Lava

Lava

Magma

Fissure volcanoes are places where floods of lava pour out of long cracks in the ground.

Shield volcanoes are shaped like upturned shields. They erupt runny lava, which spreads over a wide area.

Pyroclasts

Ash cloud

Layers of earlier eruptions

Cinder cones are built up from ash, with little lava.

Composite volcanoes are cone shaped. They build up in layers of ash and lava from a succession of explosive eruptions.

KINDS OF ERUPTION
There are many different kinds of eruptions.

ICELANDIC
Under the ocean where plates are moving apart volcanoes ooze runny lava.

STROMBOLEAN
Some volcanoes spew lava and steam and fling out blobs of hot rock.

VULCANIAN
Some fling out showers of pulverized rock.

8. LAVA FLOW
Some volcanoes gush runny lava that flows far from the vent. But explosive volcanoes push out thick, sticky lava that crawls away slowly so the volcano piles up into a cone.

PLINIAN
Along margins where plates crunch together, thick and sticky magma creates the most terrifying and explosive volcanoes of all.

PELEAN
Some spew glowing avalanches of cinders and hot gas.

HAWAIIAN
Above certain hot spots, lava flows out gently much of the time.

23

6. VOLCANO BOMBS

The blast can fire out big chunks of hot rock, too. These chunks, called pyroclasts, can be bigger than coconuts, and crash down on the landscape around the volcano.

7. ROARING FIRE

Most terrifying of all are pyroclastic flows. These are avalanches of pyroclasts, ash and gases that roar down the volcano faster than a jet plane. They are so hot they instantly burn up anything in their way.

Plug

Magma

Lava

Pyroclastic flow

WHY DO EARTHQUAKES HAPPEN?

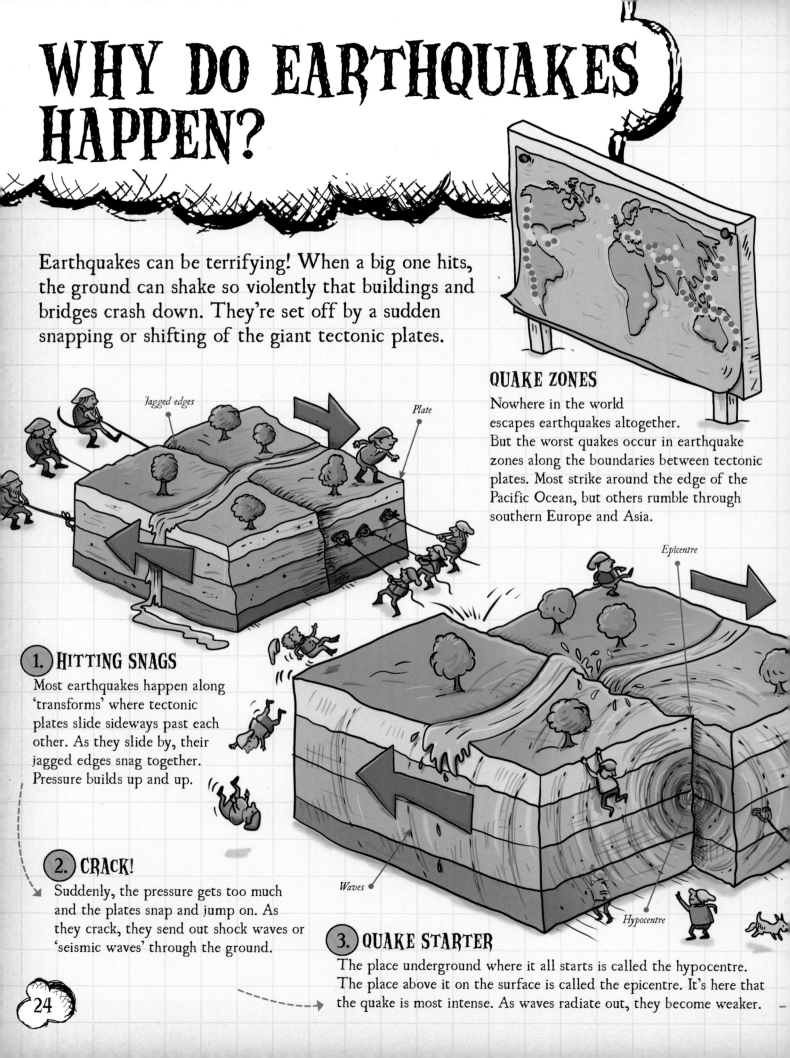

Earthquakes can be terrifying! When a big one hits, the ground can shake so violently that buildings and bridges crash down. They're set off by a sudden snapping or shifting of the giant tectonic plates.

Jagged edges

Plate

QUAKE ZONES

Nowhere in the world escapes earthquakes altogether. But the worst quakes occur in earthquake zones along the boundaries between tectonic plates. Most strike around the edge of the Pacific Ocean, but others rumble through southern Europe and Asia.

Epicentre

1. HITTING SNAGS

Most earthquakes happen along 'transforms' where tectonic plates slide sideways past each other. As they slide by, their jagged edges snag together. Pressure builds up and up.

2. CRACK!

Suddenly, the pressure gets too much and the plates snap and jump on. As they crack, they send out shock waves or 'seismic waves' through the ground.

Waves

Hypocentre

3. QUAKE STARTER

The place underground where it all starts is called the hypocentre. The place above it on the surface is called the epicentre. It's here that the quake is most intense. As waves radiate out, they become weaker.

MEASURING EARTHQUAKES

Earthquake scientists use seismometers to register quake waves. In the past, they'd rate them on the Richter scale from 0 to 9, the strongest. But for the biggest earthquakes, they now use the Moment Magnitude scale. This combines Richter readings with observations of how rocks move to reveal the true power of an earthquake.

Seismometer   *Waves*

7. GROUNDBREAKING

Earthquakes can also open up giant cracks, and throw the ground sideways or up or down, or start avalanches.

8. WOBBLY

If earthquakes hit sandy ground, they can turn it fluid so that waves can be seen rippling across them like waves in the sea. These waves can capsize tall buildings.

6. ROLLERS

The last waves to arrive travel on the surface, rolling the rock like ocean waves. These do the most damage.

Surface waves

5. SNAKY AND ROPY

The slower S or Secondary waves strike a few seconds later, shaking the ground from side to side like a snake or up and down like a flicked skipping rope.

Secondary waves

4. PUSH ME, PULL YOU

The fastest waves, called P or Primary waves, push and pull the ground deep down, squeezing and stretching it to and fro. They roar along at nearly 5 kilometres a second. When a quake hits, they are the first to arrive.

Primary waves

25

HOW ARE MOUNTAINS RAISED UP?

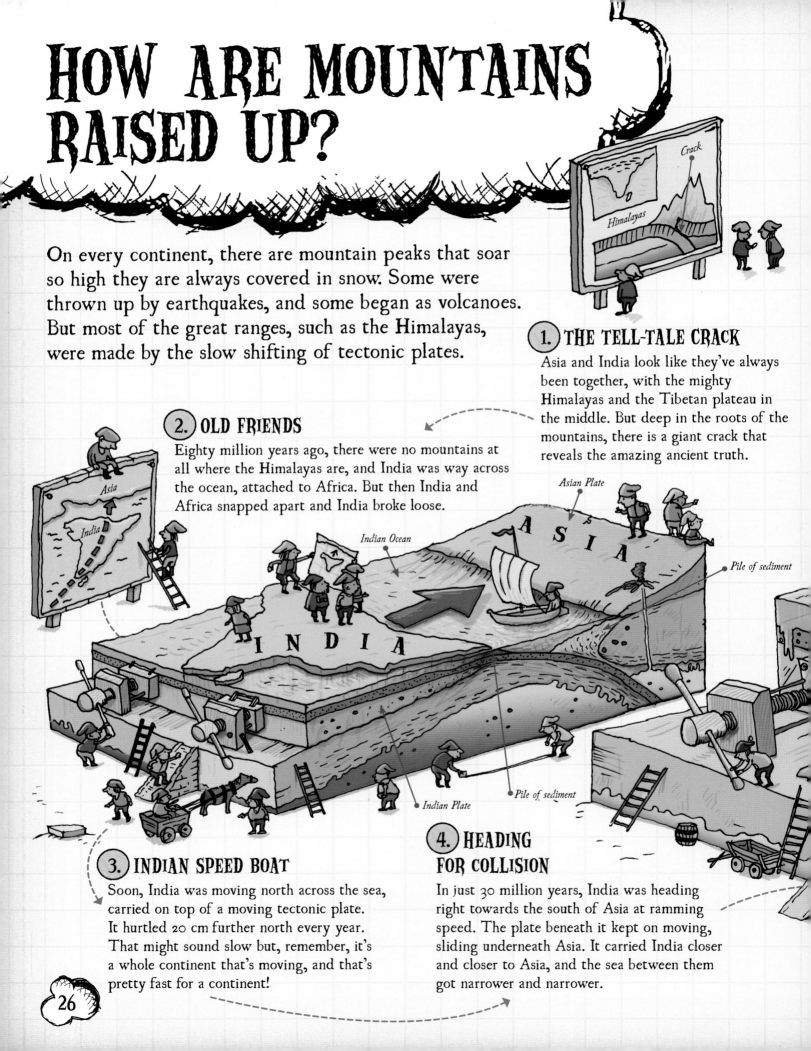

On every continent, there are mountain peaks that soar so high they are always covered in snow. Some were thrown up by earthquakes, and some began as volcanoes. But most of the great ranges, such as the Himalayas, were made by the slow shifting of tectonic plates.

1. THE TELL-TALE CRACK

Asia and India look like they've always been together, with the mighty Himalayas and the Tibetan plateau in the middle. But deep in the roots of the mountains, there is a giant crack that reveals the amazing ancient truth.

2. OLD FRIENDS

Eighty million years ago, there were no mountains at all where the Himalayas are, and India was way across the ocean, attached to Africa. But then India and Africa snapped apart and India broke loose.

3. INDIAN SPEED BOAT

Soon, India was moving north across the sea, carried on top of a moving tectonic plate. It hurtled 20 cm further north every year. That might sound slow but, remember, it's a whole continent that's moving, and that's pretty fast for a continent!

4. HEADING FOR COLLISION

In just 30 million years, India was heading right towards the south of Asia at ramming speed. The plate beneath it kept on moving, sliding underneath Asia. It carried India closer and closer to Asia, and the sea between them got narrower and narrower.

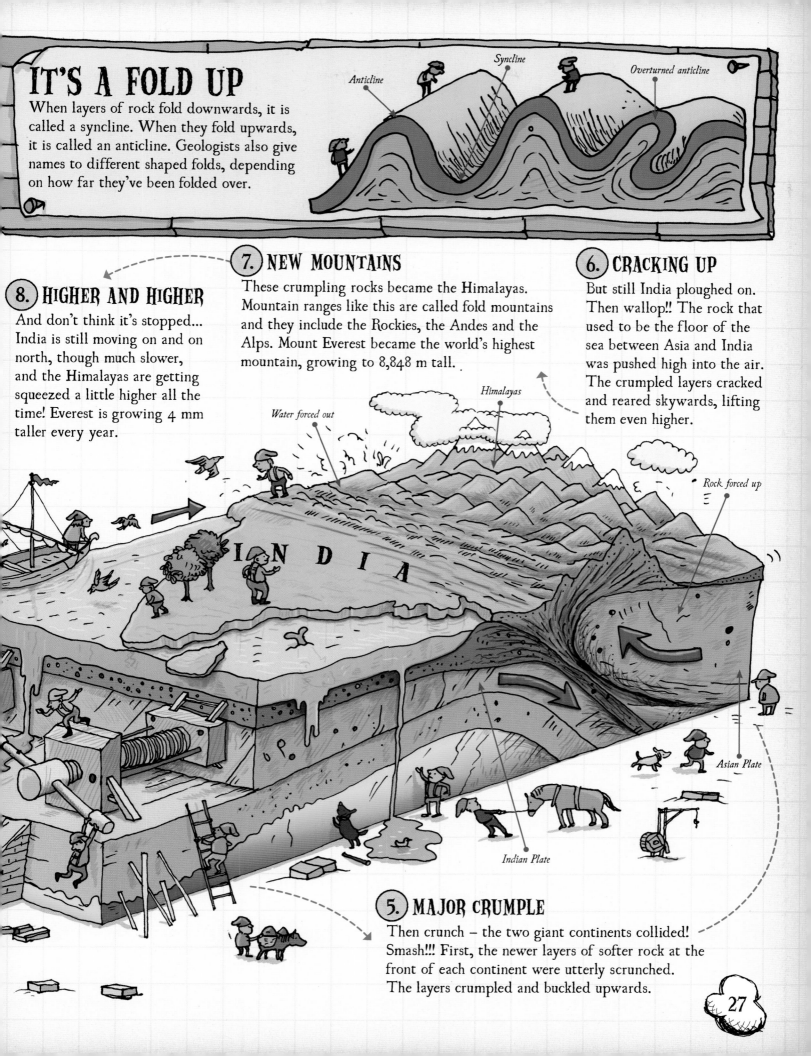

IT'S A FOLD UP

When layers of rock fold downwards, it is called a syncline. When they fold upwards, it is called an anticline. Geologists also give names to different shaped folds, depending on how far they've been folded over.

Anticline

Syncline

Overturned anticline

7. NEW MOUNTAINS

These crumpling rocks became the Himalayas. Mountain ranges like this are called fold mountains and they include the Rockies, the Andes and the Alps. Mount Everest became the world's highest mountain, growing to 8,848 m tall.

6. CRACKING UP

But still India ploughed on. Then wallop!! The rock that used to be the floor of the sea between Asia and India was pushed high into the air. The crumpled layers cracked and reared skywards, lifting them even higher.

8. HIGHER AND HIGHER

And don't think it's stopped... India is still moving on and on north, though much slower, and the Himalayas are getting squeezed a little higher all the time! Everest is growing 4 mm taller every year.

Water forced out

Himalayas

Rock forced up

INDIA

Asian Plate

Indian Plate

5. MAJOR CRUMPLE

Then crunch – the two giant continents collided! Smash!!! First, the newer layers of softer rock at the front of each continent were utterly scrunched. The layers crumpled and buckled upwards.

27

HOW DOES THE LAND WEAR DOWN?

The landscape around you is never the same for long. You may not see it change much in your lifetime, but the Earth has plenty of time. Over millions of years, even the highest, toughest mountains are beaten down by the weather and worn flat.

Rain

Wind

Valley

Scree

1. WEATHER-BEATEN

In the harsh mountain weather, battering rain and wind softens the toughest rock. Water seeps into tiny cracks and then expands as it freezes in the chilly mountain air, shattering the rock. This assault is called weathering, and it makes peaks jagged and broken.

2. MOUNTAIN RUBBLE

Fragments of weathered rock tumble down the mountain in landslides, piling up at the foot and forming rubble heaps called 'scree'.

3. WATER WORN

Rain works on the rocks, wearing them away. As it flows down the hillsides, it gathers into rivers that carry away rocks and stones. This is called erosion. Frozen water also plays a part as massive glaciers scour away at the sides of valleys removing huge amounts of rock.

MOUNTAIN COMEBACK

The mountains may have been worn flat, and their crumbled remains broken to sand, but they have not vanished altogether. That sand will, in time, form new rocks, and these rocks may then be raised by the tectonic movements of the Earth to form new mountains.

New mountains

Upthrust pushes up new mountains

6. PLAIN END

After millions of years, the hills between valleys are worn almost entirely away. The mountains are long gone, and the river winds or 'meanders' this way and that over a plain formed mostly of their crumbled, sandy remains.

Sediment

Plain

5. WIDER AND WIDER

As tributary streams flow into the river, they gradually wear away the valley sides, helped by the weather and by landslides. Over very long periods of time – hundreds of thousands of years – the valley gets broader and flatter until the river is winding over a wide plain.

4. DEEP VALLEYS

Rivers running over the same course again and again gradually wear the rock beneath away. It's a slow process, but, in time, the water carves down into the rock to create deep winding valleys, with every bend following the course of the river.

29

HOW DOES A RIVER MOVE?

Most rivers start high in the mountains as a trickle. But as they run down towards the sea, one tiny stream meets another, and another, and another. Their waters combine until, at last, they become a broad river.

STEEP AND TUMBLING

High up in the mountains, rivers are steep and narrow, tumbling this way and that over rocks. Sometimes they surge in white foam through rocks as rapids. Sometimes they plunge over ledges as waterfalls, or they just swirl around in rock pools.

1. A STREAM'S LOAD

As it flows downhill, every stream carries a load of debris or 'sediment' with it. Larger rocks and stones are rolled or bounced along the bed. Smaller grains called gravel at them, smoothing the silt float along in the water. These smaller grains are often carried all the way to sea.

2. NATURAL SCULPTORS

Streams wear away, or 'erode', their banks and beds by hurling gravel at them, smoothing the slope of their rough bed into a gentle curve. Over a long time, river erosion carves out deep valleys and shapes the land into rounded hills.

Waterfall

Pool

Rapids

Silt

Stones

Large rocks

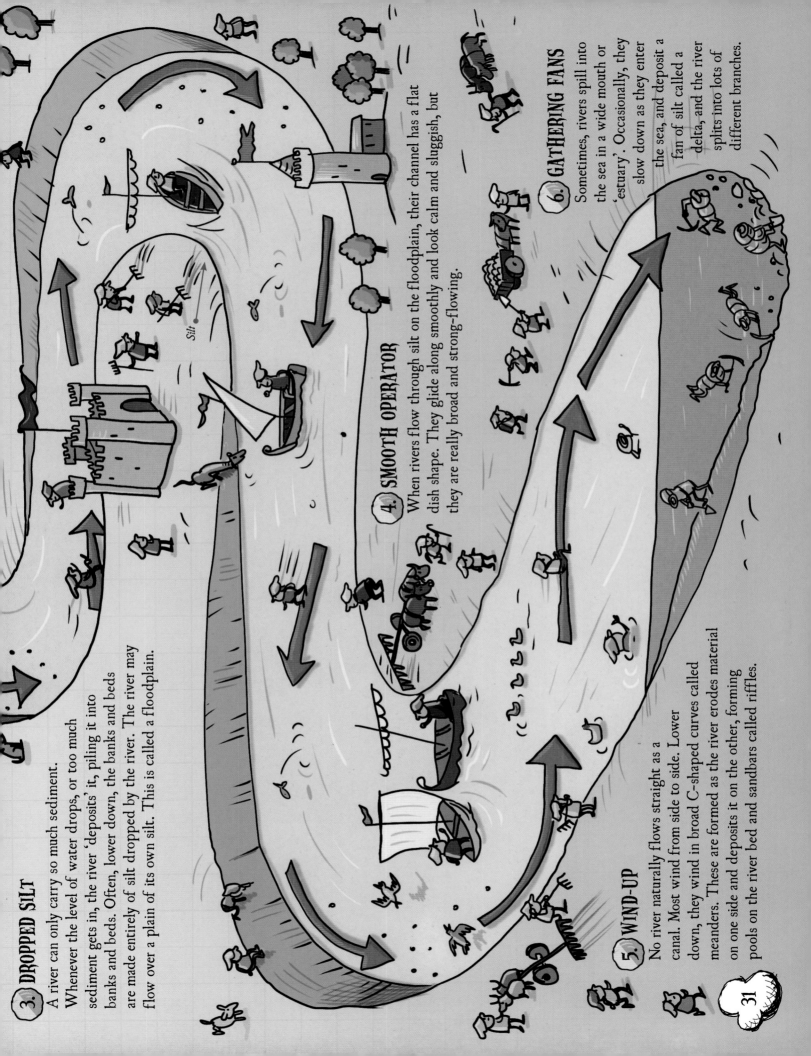

3. DROPPED SILT

A river can only carry so much sediment. Whenever the level of water drops, or too much sediment gets in, the river 'deposits' it, piling it into banks and beds. Often, lower down, the banks and beds are made entirely of silt dropped by the river. The river may flow over a plain of its own silt. This is called a floodplain.

4. SMOOTH OPERATOR

When rivers flow through silt on the floodplain, their channel has a flat dish shape. They glide along smoothly and look calm and sluggish, but they are really broad and strong-flowing.

5. WIND-UP

No river naturally flows straight as a canal. Most wind from side to side. Lower down, they wind in broad C-shaped curves called meanders. These are formed as the river erodes material on one side and deposits it on the other, forming pools on the river bed and sandbars called riffles.

6. GATHERING FANS

Sometimes, rivers spill into the sea in a wide mouth or 'estuary'. Occasionally, they slow down as they enter the sea, and deposit a fan of silt called a delta, and the river splits into lots of different branches.

Silt

31

HOW DO GLACIERS CHANGE THE LANDSCAPE?

Long ago, the world went through bleak and chilly times called Ice Ages. During these times, many valleys were filled with massive rivers of ice called glaciers. As they slithered along, these ice giants excavated the landscape.

ICE FRONT

The last Ice Age began two million years ago, and finally ended 10,000 years ago. During this time, vast sheets of ice extended south into Russia and Europe, and across North America as far as Indiana and Illinois. New Zealand and parts of South America were buried in ice, too.

Snow

Cirque

Abrasion

1. THE SNOW FIELD

Glaciers begin as snow piles up in mountain hollows, which compacts into a dish of ice. In time, so much ice builds up that it slips out of the hollow and begins to slide downhill.

2. ON THE SLIDE

Sometimes, the underside of the glacier melts, and it slides on water. Sometimes, layers in the ice slide over each other like a pack of cards.

5. THE OGRE'S ARMCHAIR

The hollow where the glacier began is dug into a deep armchair in the mountain called a cirque. The back of the chair may be worn back so far it starts to meet another, leaving a knife-sharp ridge or 'arete' between them.

6. THE GIANT'S BATHTUB

V-shaped river valleys are carved straight and broad into vast, U-shaped troughs as the ice ploughs right through the winding hills. Side valleys are often cut off entirely and left hanging, so that streams plunge from them in towering waterfalls.

7. LEFTOVERS

As the ice melts, it dumps the debris of rock it carried in piles on the valley floor, called moraines. Terminal moraines are left where the glacier's front or 'nose' once was. Lateral moraines are left along the side.

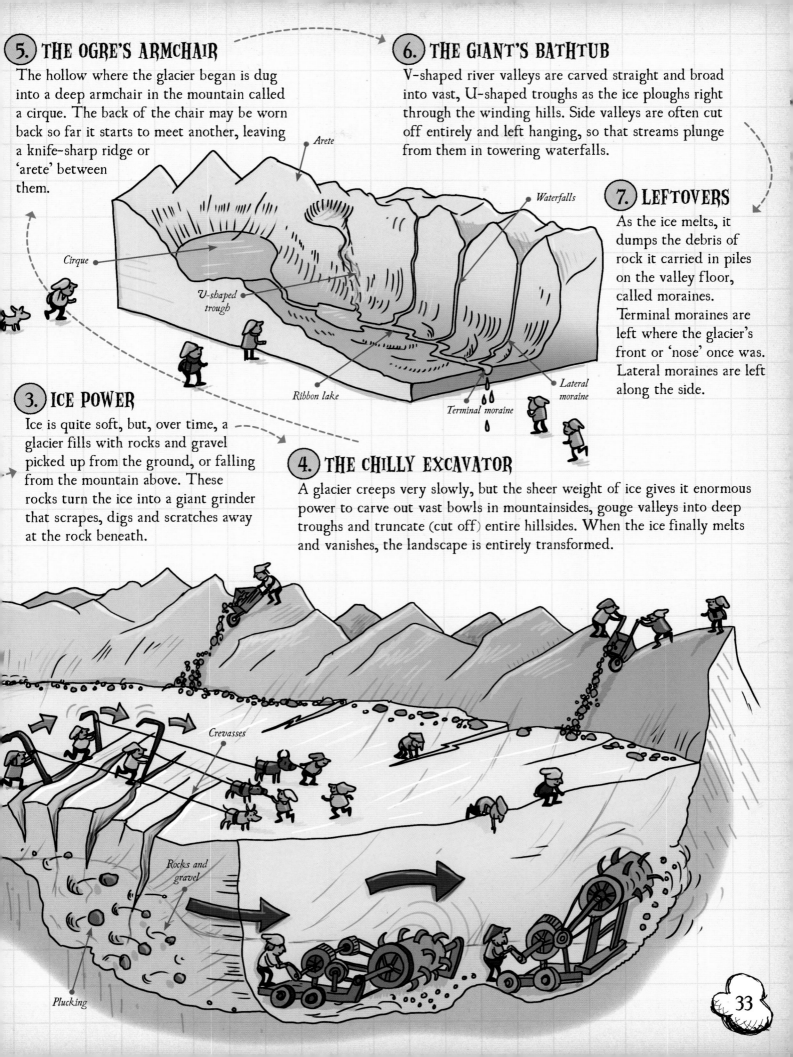

Arete

Waterfalls

Cirque

U-shaped trough

Ribbon lake

Terminal moraine

Lateral moraine

3. ICE POWER

Ice is quite soft, but, over time, a glacier fills with rocks and gravel picked up from the ground, or falling from the mountain above. These rocks turn the ice into a giant grinder that scrapes, digs and scratches away at the rock beneath.

4. THE CHILLY EXCAVATOR

A glacier creeps very slowly, but the sheer weight of ice gives it enormous power to carve out vast bowls in mountainsides, gouge valleys into deep troughs and truncate (cut off) entire hillsides. When the ice finally melts and vanishes, the landscape is entirely transformed.

Crevasses

Rocks and gravel

Plucking

33

4. ROCK CRUMBLER

Igneous rock is tough, but after millions of years of exposure to the weather, it crumbles to bits. The bits become pebbles, sand and gravel, and are washed down by rivers to the sea to settle as 'sediments', or piled up by the wind in deserts.

SEDIMENTARY ROCKS

Pebbles, sand and gravel

Layers of sediment

5. LAYER BUILDER

Sediments pile on each other, and each buried layer is squeezed hard. Over millions of years, they are buried deeper and squeezed harder, and cooked by Earth's warm interior, eventually becoming layers of sedimentary rock.

Mountains

6. MAGMA AND MOUNTAINS

The shifting of Earth's surface means sedimentary layers are rarely left in peace. Some are swept down into Earth's hot interior, where they melt to form new igneous rocks. Some are thrown up as mountains, that are crumbled in time by the weather to form new sediments.

Swept back down

MAGMA

HOW ARE ROCKS MADE?

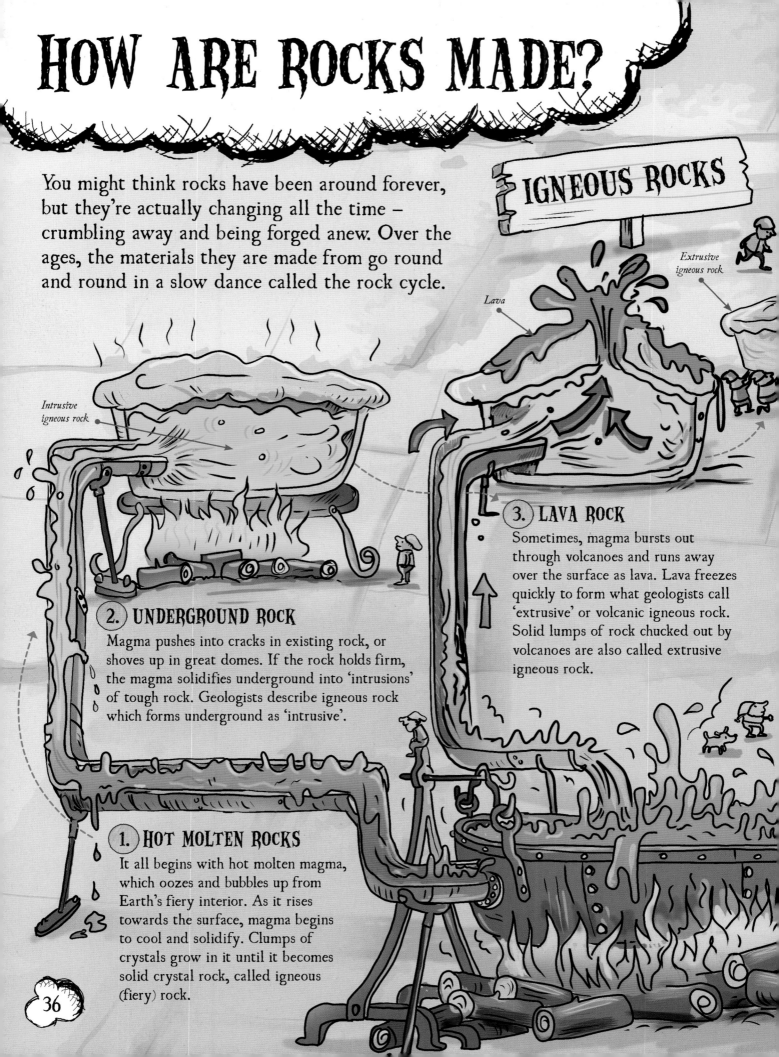

You might think rocks have been around forever, but they're actually changing all the time – crumbling away and being forged anew. Over the ages, the materials they are made from go round and round in a slow dance called the rock cycle.

IGNEOUS ROCKS

Extrusive igneous rock

Lava

Intrusive igneous rock

3. LAVA ROCK

Sometimes, magma bursts out through volcanoes and runs away over the surface as lava. Lava freezes quickly to form what geologists call 'extrusive' or volcanic igneous rock. Solid lumps of rock chucked out by volcanoes are also called extrusive igneous rock.

2. UNDERGROUND ROCK

Magma pushes into cracks in existing rock, or shoves up in great domes. If the rock holds firm, the magma solidifies underground into 'intrusions' of tough rock. Geologists describe igneous rock which forms underground as 'intrusive'.

1. HOT MOLTEN ROCKS

It all begins with hot molten magma, which oozes and bubbles up from Earth's fiery interior. As it rises towards the surface, magma begins to cool and solidify. Clumps of crystals grow in it until it becomes solid crystal rock, called igneous (fiery) rock.

HOW ARE CAVES DUG OUT?

Deep underground, strange natural palaces have been carved out of rock, pitch dark and silent, except for the echoing drip of water. Most of these caverns are small, but some are as big as cathedrals, and feature amazing natural spires and hanging spikes.

1. ROCK BLOCKS

The biggest caverns of all are in limestone rock. When limestone forms, it cracks into giant blocks and is criss-crossed with cracks between them, known as 'joints'. Where the blocks are exposed on the surface, they look like paving stones or giant bricks.

2. VANISHING WATER

Streams vanish into the cracks. There are holes in the rock, which are called swallowholes because it looks like a stream has been swallowed up! Really big swallowholes that look big enough to gulp down rivers are called ponors.

3. WASH DOWN

Sometimes, water gathers into underground streams and can bubble out of the ground at a spring much lower down. Sometimes, it pools up in the lower layers of the rock. In places where the rock is hollow, it forms eerie underground lakes.

4. DISSOLVING ROCK

Carbon dioxide gas from the air makes rain mildly acid. Amazingly, it's just acidic enough to dissolve limestone rock, like water dissolves sugar. So wherever water trickles down through the ground, it etches rock away.

Joints

Swallowholes

Tunnel

Dissolving rock

Stream

Stalagmite

Underground lake

8.) GLISTENING SPIKES

Sometimes, water drips right down onto the floor. As it drips in the same place again and again, the dissolved rock may build a spike pointing up towards the roof. This is called a stalagmite. Shiny stalactites and stalagmites and other drip features turn the cavern into a glistening palace.

7.) BIG DRIPS

In some caverns, water trickling through the rocks drips from the roof. As it drips, it may leave behind some of the rock dissolved in it. This can build up to form a fantastic spike that hangs like an icicle. It is called a stalactite.

9.) COLLAPSE

Eventually, so much rock in the roof of the cavern may be dissolved away that it entirely collapses. Then the entire cavern is open to the sky. When a whole network of caverns collapses, it may become a gorge.

6.) SECRET PASSAGES

Some caves are just a big single space. But many are wonderful labyrinths of caves linked by tunnels, some underwater. It takes a brave caver to explore these dark underground spaces.

Gorge

Stalactite

Cavern

5.) WIDER AND WIDER

As the rock dissolves away, swallowholes and underground spaces get bigger and bigger. In time, these spaces open up to form caves, or even bigger caves called caverns. Over tens of thousands of years, caverns can grow as big as cathedrals.

Spring

35

ROCK RECIPE

Rocks are made from crystals of natural chemicals called minerals or, occasionally, the compacted remains of living things. With some rocks, the grains are so tiny, you can only see them under a microscope.

Sandstone

Basalt

Sedimentary rocks, such as sandstone, are pale and dull-coloured and made from grains cemented together – which rub off if you rub them against another rock.

Marble

Granite

Schist

Igneous rocks, such as granite and basalt, usually have a hard, shiny, mottled look. With a magnifying glass, you can see that the crystals interlock like a jigsaw.

Metamorphic rocks, such as marble and schist, are typically glittery and feel smooth, and often have stripes.

HOW DOES THE OCEAN MOVE?

The world's oceans are never still, and it's not just the surface that moves. Deep down, the entire ocean is turning over slowly in great spirals, moving water as if on a giant conveyor belt.

DOWN

GREENLAND

7. VIKING WATER
It takes a millennium or more for water to go right around. So water just coming back to Greenland now began its epic journey in the time of the Vikings – but the amount of water involved is awesome.

6. HEADING NORTH
The surface currents flow on westwards round the south of Africa and into the Atlantic. There, they flow north while deep down the cold current flows in the opposite direction. At last, the waters reach the north, to complete the journey.

1. DEEP AND CHILLY
In the icy seas of the North Atlantic, the water gets very chilly, so chilly that some freezes. That leaves the water that doesn't freeze super salty – so cold and heavy that it sinks deep down to the bottom of the ocean floor.

NORTH ATLANTIC

NORTH AMERICA

SOUTH AMERICA

SOUTH ATLANTIC

2. OOZING IN THE DARK
The cold water oozes south along the ocean floor. Nobody can see it moving down there in the dark, but it is creeping ever south, pushed on by water sinking behind. In time, it creeps right along the Atlantic to the far south of the world.

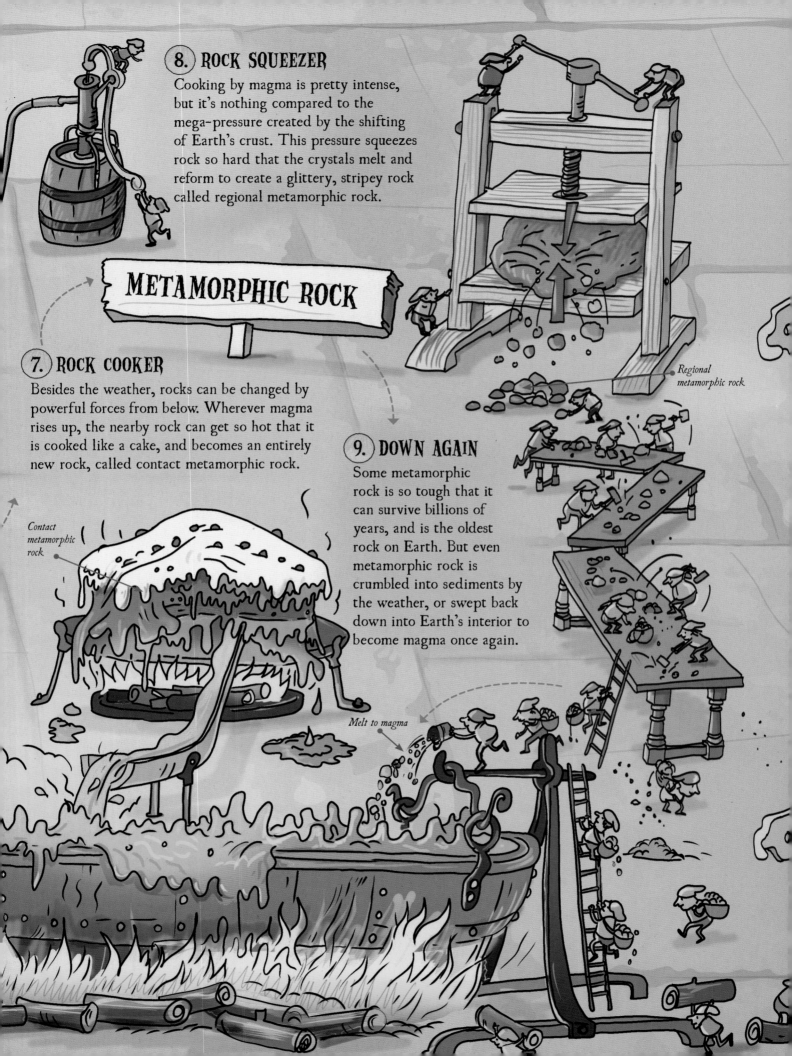

8. ROCK SQUEEZER

Cooking by magma is pretty intense, but it's nothing compared to the mega-pressure created by the shifting of Earth's crust. This pressure squeezes rock so hard that the crystals melt and reform to create a glittery, stripey rock called regional metamorphic rock.

METAMORPHIC ROCK

7. ROCK COOKER

Besides the weather, rocks can be changed by powerful forces from below. Wherever magma rises up, the nearby rock can get so hot that it is cooked like a cake, and becomes an entirely new rock, called contact metamorphic rock.

Regional metamorphic rock

9. DOWN AGAIN

Some metamorphic rock is so tough that it can survive billions of years, and is the oldest rock on Earth. But even metamorphic rock is crumbled into sediments by the weather, or swept back down into Earth's interior to become magma once again.

Contact metamorphic rock

Melt to magma

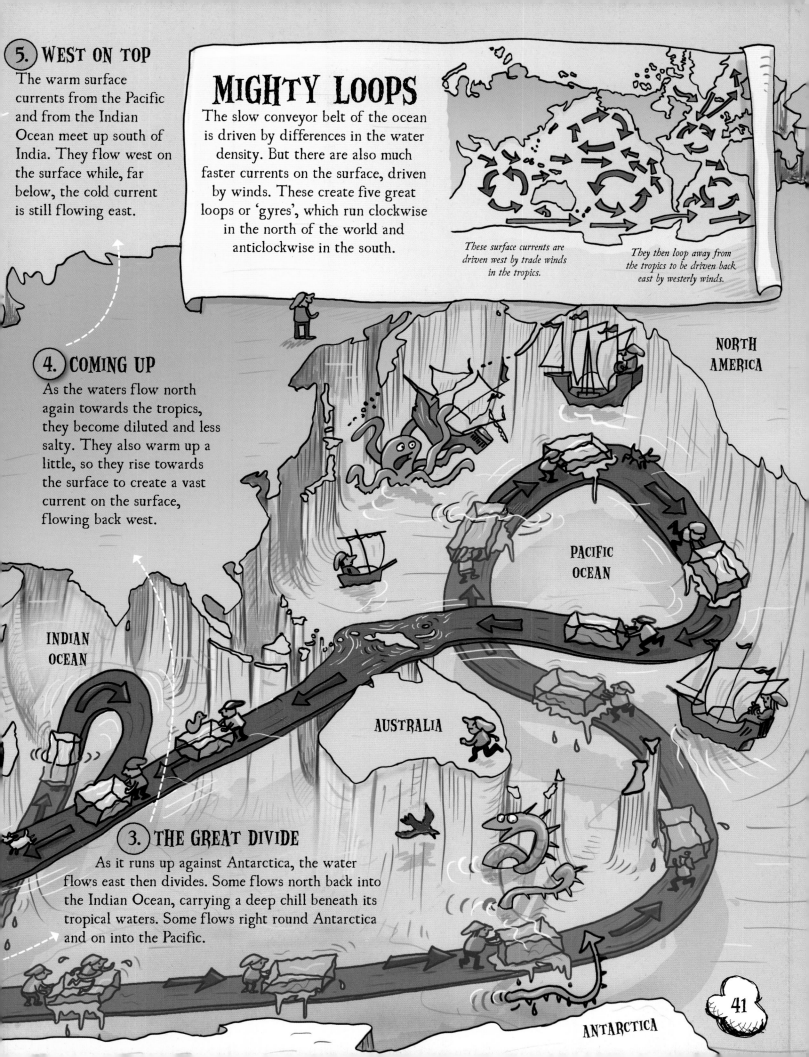

5. WEST ON TOP

The warm surface currents from the Pacific and from the Indian Ocean meet up south of India. They flow west on the surface while, far below, the cold current is still flowing east.

MIGHTY LOOPS

The slow conveyor belt of the ocean is driven by differences in the water density. But there are also much faster currents on the surface, driven by winds. These create five great loops or 'gyres', which run clockwise in the north of the world and anticlockwise in the south.

These surface currents are driven west by trade winds in the tropics.

They then loop away from the tropics to be driven back east by westerly winds.

4. COMING UP

As the waters flow north again towards the tropics, they become diluted and less salty. They also warm up a little, so they rise towards the surface to create a vast current on the surface, flowing back west.

3. THE GREAT DIVIDE

As it runs up against Antarctica, the water flows east then divides. Some flows north back into the Indian Ocean, carrying a deep chill beneath its tropical waters. Some flows right round Antarctica and on into the Pacific.

NORTH AMERICA

PACIFIC OCEAN

INDIAN OCEAN

AUSTRALIA

ANTARCTICA

HOW DO WAVES SHAPE COASTS?

If you go to the seaside, you see waves hurling themselves at the shore. They may lap gently or tear in ferociously, wearing down the toughest cliffs into sandy beaches.

WHEN THE WEATHER IS MILD...

1. WHERE THE WINDS BLOW

Far out on the ocean, strong winds blow over the water, whipping the ocean surface into ripples that pile up to form rolling waves. These waves are called swell because they make the ocean rise and fall.

Wind

Rollers

Swell

Ripples

2. RISE AND FALL

Waves can run far across the ocean, but the water in them really just swells up and down and barely moves. Imagine a Mexican wave going round a sports stadium, with the spectators getting up then sitting down again.

3. ROLLING, ROLLING

Inside each wave, the water rolls round as it swells up, which is why waves are sometimes called rollers. Sometimes, an extra strong wind whips water off the top, or crest, into white foam.

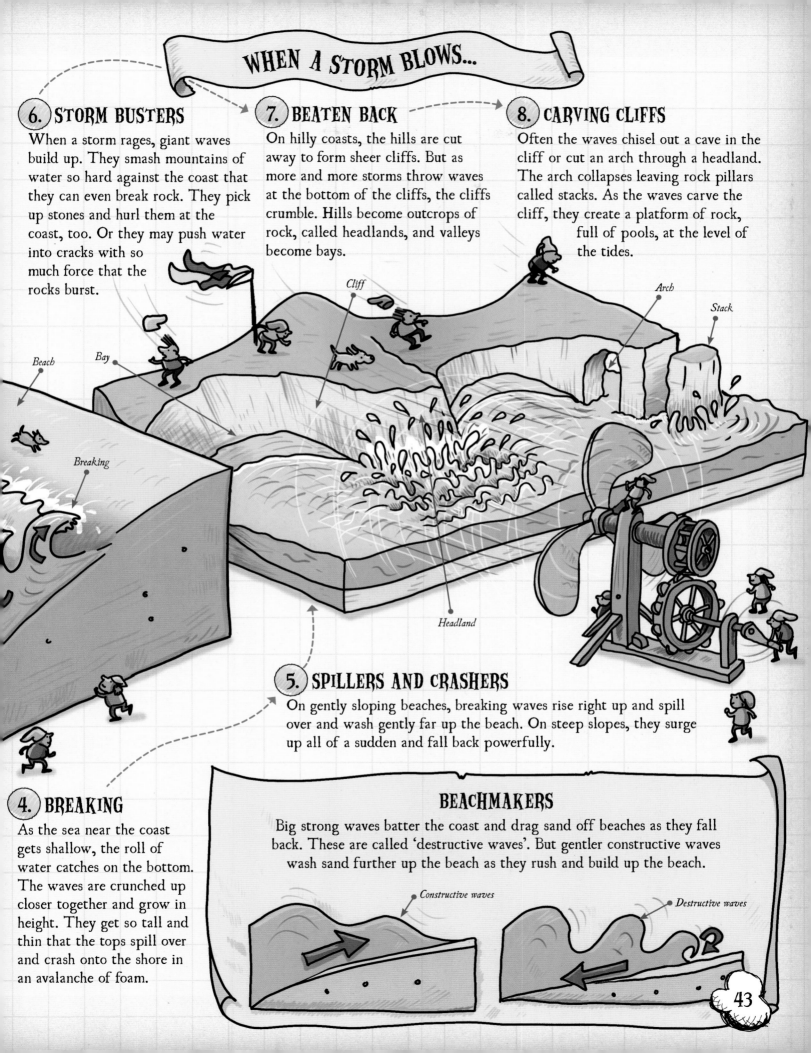

WHEN A STORM BLOWS...

6. STORM BUSTERS

When a storm rages, giant waves build up. They smash mountains of water so hard against the coast that they can even break rock. They pick up stones and hurl them at the coast, too. Or they may push water into cracks with so much force that the rocks burst.

7. BEATEN BACK

On hilly coasts, the hills are cut away to form sheer cliffs. But as more and more storms throw waves at the bottom of the cliffs, the cliffs crumble. Hills become outcrops of rock, called headlands, and valleys become bays.

8. CARVING CLIFFS

Often the waves chisel out a cave in the cliff or cut an arch through a headland. The arch collapses leaving rock pillars called stacks. As the waves carve the cliff, they create a platform of rock, full of pools, at the level of the tides.

Cliff

Beach

Bay

Breaking

Arch

Stack

Headland

5. SPILLERS AND CRASHERS

On gently sloping beaches, breaking waves rise right up and spill over and wash gently far up the beach. On steep slopes, they surge up all of a sudden and fall back powerfully.

4. BREAKING

As the sea near the coast gets shallow, the roll of water catches on the bottom. The waves are crunched up closer together and grow in height. They get so tall and thin that the tops spill over and crash onto the shore in an avalanche of foam.

BEACHMAKERS

Big strong waves batter the coast and drag sand off beaches as they fall back. These are called 'destructive waves'. But gentler constructive waves wash sand further up the beach as they rush and build up the beach.

Constructive waves

Destructive waves

43

WHAT'S IN THE AIR?

The Earth is wrapped in a blanket of gases called the atmosphere. You can't see it, but it is made of lots of layers and many gases, including water vapour. Sometimes, though, the water vapour turns into water drops and ice crystals, painting an ever-changing gallery of clouds.

HIGH CLOUDS

Cirrus

Cirrocumulus

1. HORSES' MANES

Cirrus clouds form very high up. It's so cold up here they are made entirely of ice, blown into curly wisps like hair or horses' manes. They sparkle brilliant white in the sunshine and warn that a storm is on its way.

2. FISHY SKIES

Occasionally, gusty air mixes 'supercooled' water in with ice crystals and piles cirrus clouds into ripples. The ripples look so like fish scales that they're sometimes called mackerel skies. It's fine now, but maybe stormy soon!

Cirrostratus

3. SILKY VEILS

Sometimes, rising air can spread out a thin veil of ice crystals across the sky, forming cirrostratus clouds. These are so thin that you can't always see them; they just make the sky pale, and the sun may have a halo where it shines through. Look for drizzle tomorrow.

MID-LEVEL CLOUDS

Altostratus

5. WOOLLY BLANKETS

Altostratus look like a big woolly blanket. They form when cirrostratus clouds sink and the ice mixes with water drops. The sun shines through it so weakly and palely that you can't see any shadows. Expect a change in the weather, maybe even snow.

Altocumulus

4. CLUMPY CLOUDLETS

Altocumulus clouds form where the wind stirs into waves near mountains. They look a little like mackerel skies, but they are more broken into separate little clouds and made mostly of water drops.

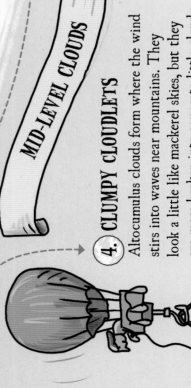

6. GLOOM CLOUDS

When altostratus thicken into nimbostratus clouds, you're in for a dull, wet day. They block out the sun, turning the sky dark grey, and often shower you with rain that just won't stop.

Nimbostratus

7. SUNNY DAY CLOUDS

Cumulus are fluffy clouds that float through the blue on a sunny day. They pile up where the sun heats the ground sending puffs of warm air up into the sky. They are white on top and pale grey underneath. Sometimes, they thicken and grow into rain clouds.

Cumulus

8. CLOUD BATH

Stratus clouds form so low that they virtually wash you in mist, or even foggy cloud. The air is so still then that they can hang around for ages, doing very little at all. Sometimes, though, they may dampen you with drizzle.

Stratus

LOW CLOUDS

Cumulonimbus

9. THUNDERHEADS

Cumulonimbus clouds are monstrous, dark grey masses that tower high into the sky. Though their base is fluffy cumulus, they are topped by icy cirrus, which is often blown out sideways to give the cloud a shape like a blacksmith's anvil. Watch out for thunder and lightning, and deluges of rain!

LAYERS OF AIR

Nearly all the air's water vapour and all the churning clouds and weather are concentrated into the atmosphere's lowest layer, called the troposphere. Above that, the atmosphere has several other layers, each with less and less air, until it all vanishes into the emptiness of space.

- **Above 700 km** *Exosphere – outermost layer*
- **300–700 km** *Ionosphere – the electrically charged layer*
- **80–300 km** *Thermosphere – sun-scorched upper layer*
- **50–80 km** *Mesosphere – chilly high level layer*
- **12–50 km** *Stratosphere – the still, calm, cloudless layer where jetplanes fly*
- **0–12 km** *Troposphere – the turbulent and cloudy weather layer*

45

WHERE DOES WATER GO?

Water is very old and came to Earth long ago – no-one knows how. But all the water in the world today – from the ocean deep to the water in your taps – is that same ancient water, used over and over again.

Heat from the Sun

Clouds

1. THE WORLD'S WATER TANK

All but a tiny bit of Earth's water sits in the oceans. And most of it has wallowed there for billions of years, just as it did when life first started on Earth. It's like a very old bath, stirring around very slowly.

2. WET AIR

But as the Sun beats down, it warms the ocean surface and makes a little water evaporate. This water seems to vanish into the air. But no – it's just invisible. The air is often wet through with evaporated water or water vapour!

Water vapour

WATERY WORDS

EVAPORATION – when liquid water warms up enough to turn to vapour.

CONDENSATION – when moist air cools, letting vapour turn back into liquid drops of water.

EVAPO-TRANSPIRATION – water oozing out of leaves, then evaporating.

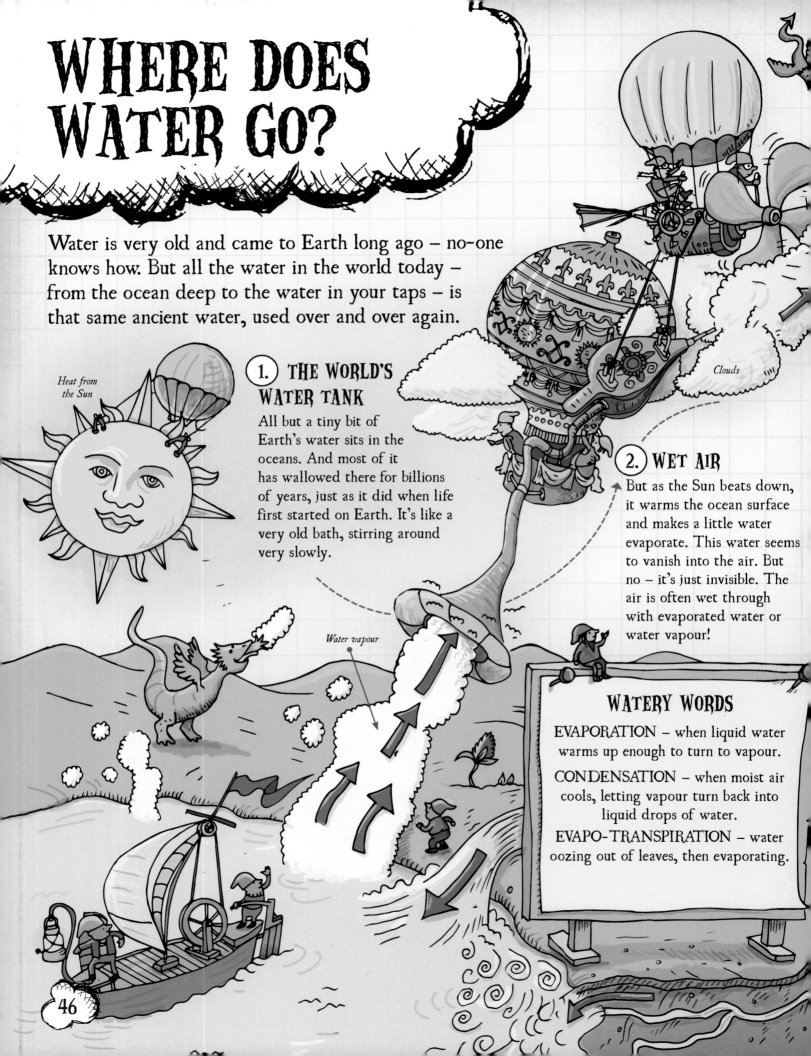

3. RISING WATER

The warm, moist air drifts up and up. But as it rises, it cools down. Then the water vapour condenses into droplets, like drops on a steamed up mirror. For a while the droplets are so tiny they float in the air as clouds.

Rain

Snow

Glaciers

4. FALLING WATER

As clouds drift through the sky, the droplets clump together and swell. Soon, they're so big and heavy that they can no longer float on the air. Then they fall as rain or snow flakes.

5. RUNNING RIVERS

Rain splashes on the ground, and runs downhill. Raindrops join to form streams, streams join to make rivers, and rivers carry the water back to the ocean.

ICE STORE

Sometimes, the air is so cold, that snow falls instead of rain. And the snow may pile up and become ice in glaciers and ice caps. These can stay frozen for tens of thousands of years before melting and returning the water to the sea.

Evaporating water

Ground water

6. WET GROUND

Some water soaks into the ground, where plants suck it up through their roots. Or it may trickle through the ground and emerge in streams lower down.

7. PLANT WATER

Plants suck water in, up through their stems to their leaves. As the Sun warms the leaves, water sweats from pores on the underside and evaporates into the air, where it rises to become clouds.

47

HOW DO RAIN STORMS HAPPEN?

All year, a dollop of cold air sits over the Arctic. It oozes south until it runs up against warm winds blowing from the tropics, forming a boundary called the polar front. It's here winter storms begin, bringing blustery winds and rain.

GETTING DEPRESSED

Winter storms start where warm air curls up over the cold, creating a wedge in the polar front called a depression, because air pressure here is reduced. The rising air piles up rain clouds, and draws strong winds in to replace it, setting off a spinning storm.

Cold air

Warm air

Depression

DOUBLE BLOW

Westerly winds drag the storm east, bringing stormy weather as each arm of the wedge passes over you. First to hit you is the "warm" front where warm air rides up over cold. Then comes the "cold" front where cold air undercuts the warm.

Cold front

Warm front

Rising warm air

1. HIGH WARNING

The first sign of an approaching storm is the wispy cirrus clouds, high at the leading edge of the warm front. If you see these coming, get ready for rain in about six hours.

2. CLOSER

Soon the sky fills with veils of cirrostratus clouds which form lower down the front and show it is beginning to move over you. Air pressure is dropping, the air is getting chillier, and the wind is stirring.

WARM FRONT

3. THE RAIN COMES DOWN

The sky darkens as it fills first with altostratus clouds then thick nimbostratus rain clouds. Soon it's drizzling, and then it's raining. It goes on raining steadily for hours as the base of the warm front passes.

6. PHEW!

Fortunately, the cold front is much steeper and passes over quickly. The worst is over in an hour or so. The rain stops and the wind drops to leave clear, cold air and a few fluffy cumulus clouds scudding through the sky.

5. STORM TIME!

Along the cold front, the cold air shoves the warm air up sharply, piling up vast and stormy thunderclouds, which burst on you ferociously. The winds veer sharply, rain comes down in torrents, and the sky may flash with lightning and roar with thunder!

4. FALSE CALM

Finally, the rain peters out, the skies seem to clear, except for some fluffy stratocumulus, and it actually seems warmer. But this is just a lull before the real action begins when the cold front hits you.

COLD FRONT

Cold air

Thunderclouds

Rising
warm air

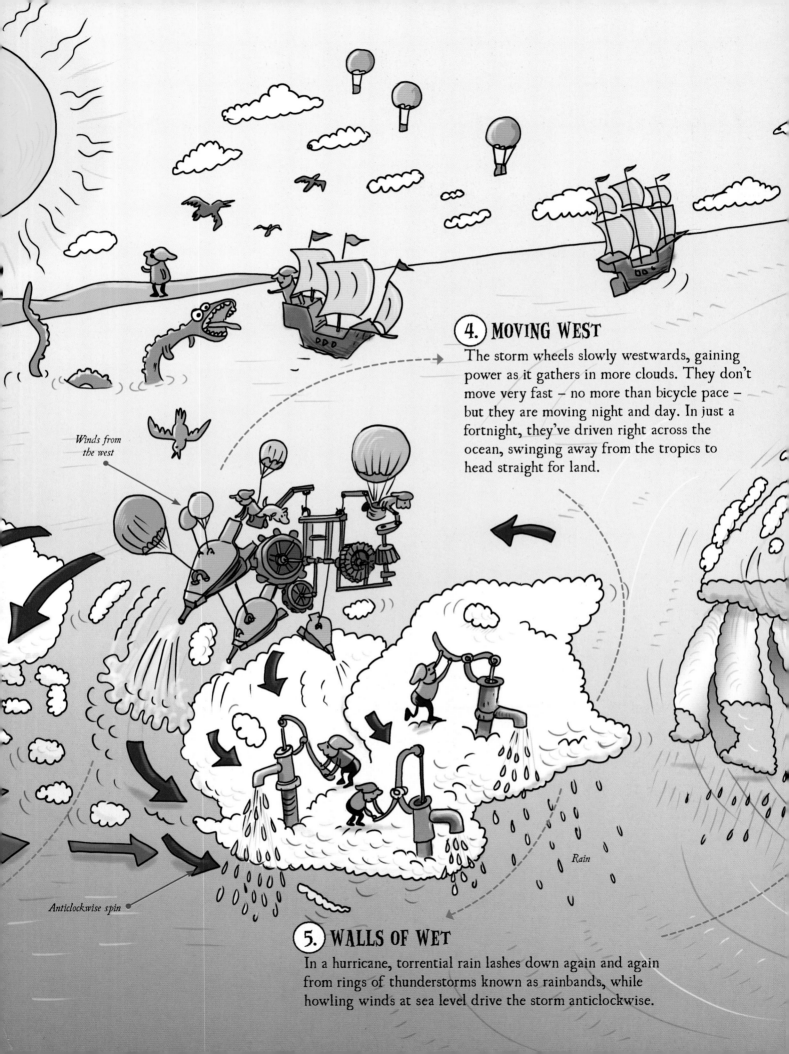

Winds from the west

4.) MOVING WEST

The storm wheels slowly westwards, gaining power as it gathers in more clouds. They don't move very fast – no more than bicycle pace – but they are moving night and day. In just a fortnight, they've driven right across the ocean, swinging away from the tropics to head straight for land.

Anticlockwise spin

Rain

5.) WALLS OF WET

In a hurricane, torrential rain lashes down again and again from rings of thunderstorms known as rainbands, while howling winds at sea level drive the storm anticlockwise.

WHY DO WINDS BLOW?

The air around you is never still. It's always on the move, blowing and flowing from places that are cool to places that are warm. Think of it like a giant wind machine that's always drawing air from the cold poles to the warm Equator.

1. TROPICAL RISING

The air in the tropics is warmed by the scorching tropical sun. As it warms, it expands and floats up. Over oceans and damp forests, it carries moisture up with it, piling up towering clouds. By mid-afternoon the clouds are a great sopping mass – so wet that they eventually unleash a brief deluge of rain.

2. GOING NORTH, GOING SOUTH

The rising air pushes air out of the way. And so air flows away either side of the Equator, high above the ground – some going north and some south. These high-level winds blow far north and south.

3. DRYING OUT

In the subtropics, thousands of kilometres from the Equator, the high-level winds cool and sink towards the ground. The air gets squeezed and warmed, like a bicycle pump when you pump hard, and dries – so dry that deserts may form here.

4. TROPICAL ROLL

Just as the air rising at the tropics pushes out high-level winds, the sinking subtropic air squeezes air back towards the Equator. This air flowing back drives steady winds, called trade winds, that blow all year in tropical areas. The air travels in a huge vertical circle, called a Hadley cell.

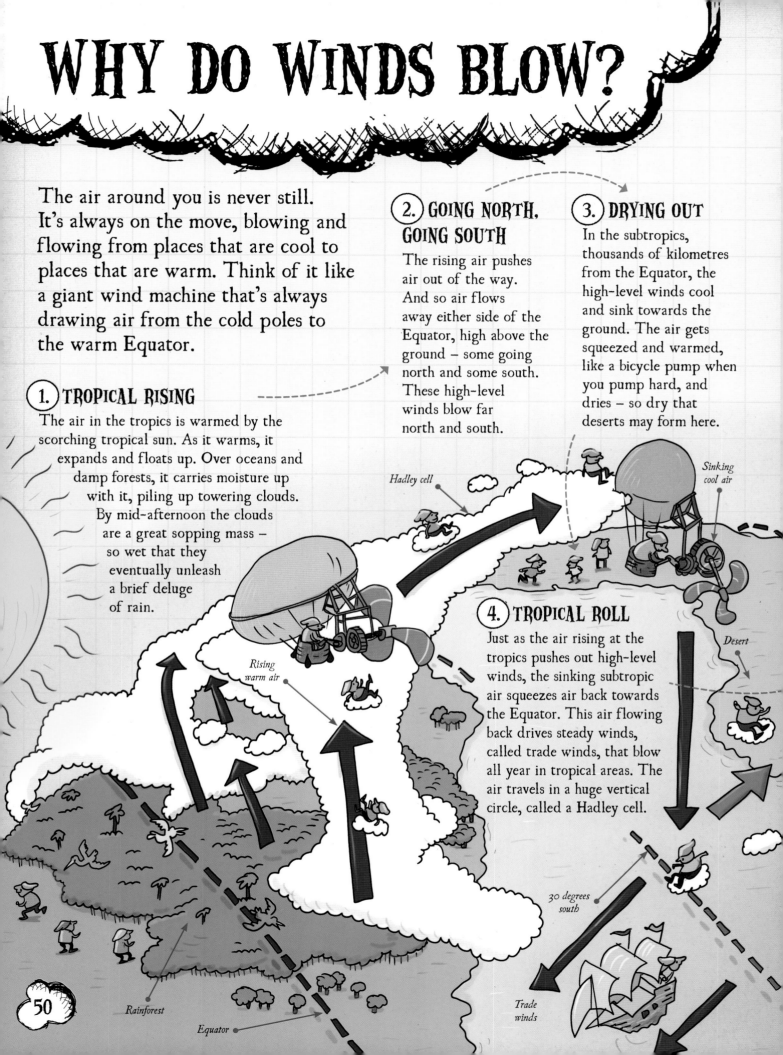

Hadley cell

Sinking cool air

Rising warm air

Desert

30 degrees south

Rainforest

Equator

Trade winds

50

HOW DO HURRICANES HAPPEN?

Hurricanes are vast tropical storms that roll in from the east across the ocean. From far, far above, they look like whirling cream cakes, but they are anything but sweet. They are whipped into whirls by roaring winds, and the cream is rings of huge thunderclouds that bring torrential rain.

Thunderclouds

1. HURRICANE NURSERIES

Hurricanes are born in late summer, just north or south of the Equator on the eastern edge of the great oceans: the Atlantic, the Indian and the Pacific. In the Atlantic, their nursery is the warm ocean off northwest Africa, near the Cape Verde Islands.

Water vapour

2. STEAMY START

The storm begins as nothing more than puffs of water vapour, wafting off the ocean as the tropical sun beats down. But there is so much sun, and so much vapour, that it soon builds up into giant thunderclouds.

Trade winds from the east

3. THE GATHERING STORM

High above, strong winds blow from the west, skimming the tops of the thunderclouds, while trade winds blow from the east across the ocean. These opposing winds twist the thunderclouds and swirl them together into one spiralling storm.

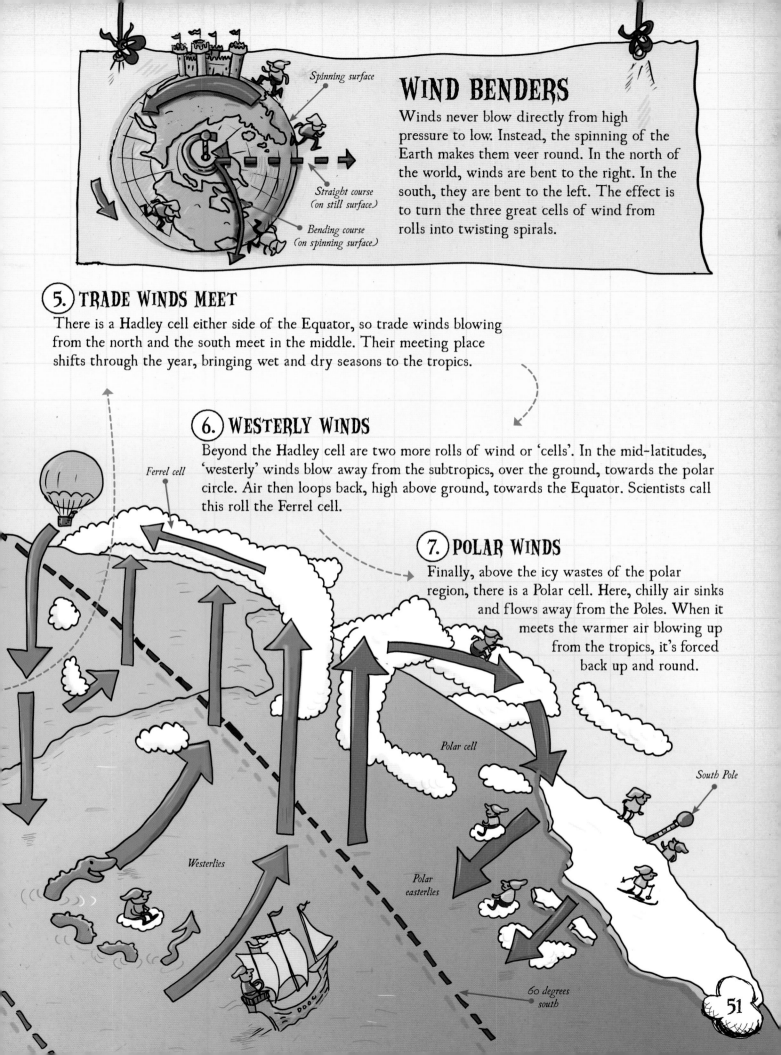

WIND BENDERS

Winds never blow directly from high pressure to low. Instead, the spinning of the Earth makes them veer round. In the north of the world, winds are bent to the right. In the south, they are bent to the left. The effect is to turn the three great cells of wind from rolls into twisting spirals.

Spinning surface

Straight course (on still surface)

Bending course (on spinning surface)

(5.) TRADE WINDS MEET

There is a Hadley cell either side of the Equator, so trade winds blowing from the north and the south meet in the middle. Their meeting place shifts through the year, bringing wet and dry seasons to the tropics.

(6.) WESTERLY WINDS

Beyond the Hadley cell are two more rolls of wind or 'cells'. In the mid-latitudes, 'westerly' winds blow away from the subtropics, over the ground, towards the polar circle. Air then loops back, high above ground, towards the Equator. Scientists call this roll the Ferrel cell.

Ferrel cell

(7.) POLAR WINDS

Finally, above the icy wastes of the polar region, there is a Polar cell. Here, chilly air sinks and flows away from the Poles. When it meets the warmer air blowing up from the tropics, it's forced back up and round.

Polar cell

South Pole

Westerlies

Polar easterlies

60 degrees south

HURRICANE FORCE

Hurricane winds blow very strong. To be classed as a hurricane, a storm must have winds of at least 118 km/h. These are known as 'hurricane force' winds. In a mighty hurricane, winds can get much stronger. In Hurricane Irma in 2017, winds gusted to 346 km/h!

8. STORM COMING!

Long before the storm arrives, huge waves stirred up by the wind start to smash against the coast. Then watchers on the shore see terrifying dark clouds heading their way. When the wind begins to pick up, you know you're in for a rough time!

9. RISING WATERS

As the storm moves over land, it loses its power and hurricane winds drop. But the torrential rain can do huge damage. For days after a hurricane passes, rivers fill up and the swollen waters can sweep away bridges and cause terrible flooding.

Surge

WHY ARE SOME PLACES SO HOT?

Everywhere in the world has its own special climate. Polar regions and mountain-tops are freezing all year round. But in the tropics, it's never cold, and it's often hot – very hot!

1. SUN POWER

The tropics are hot because it's here that the Sun shines on the Earth most directly. Or rather it's here that the Earth faces the Sun full on, so sunlight is very concentrated.

2. HIGH NOON

From the ground in the tropics, you can see the Sun climb quickly in the sky every day. By midday, it's almost directly overhead. But night comes quickly, too. In the tropics, night and day are much the same length.

3. TROPICAL THUNDER

In moist, tropical areas, rising temperatures in the morning lift moisture into the air, building up huge thunderclouds. By mid-afternoon, things are really hotting up, and clouds are ready to unleash storms.

4. THE MILD ZONE

The temperate zone is the middling zone between the tropic and polar regions. Here, the Earth is more angled to the Sun, so its heat is more spread out. The weather is generally cooler, especially in winter, though summers can be hot.

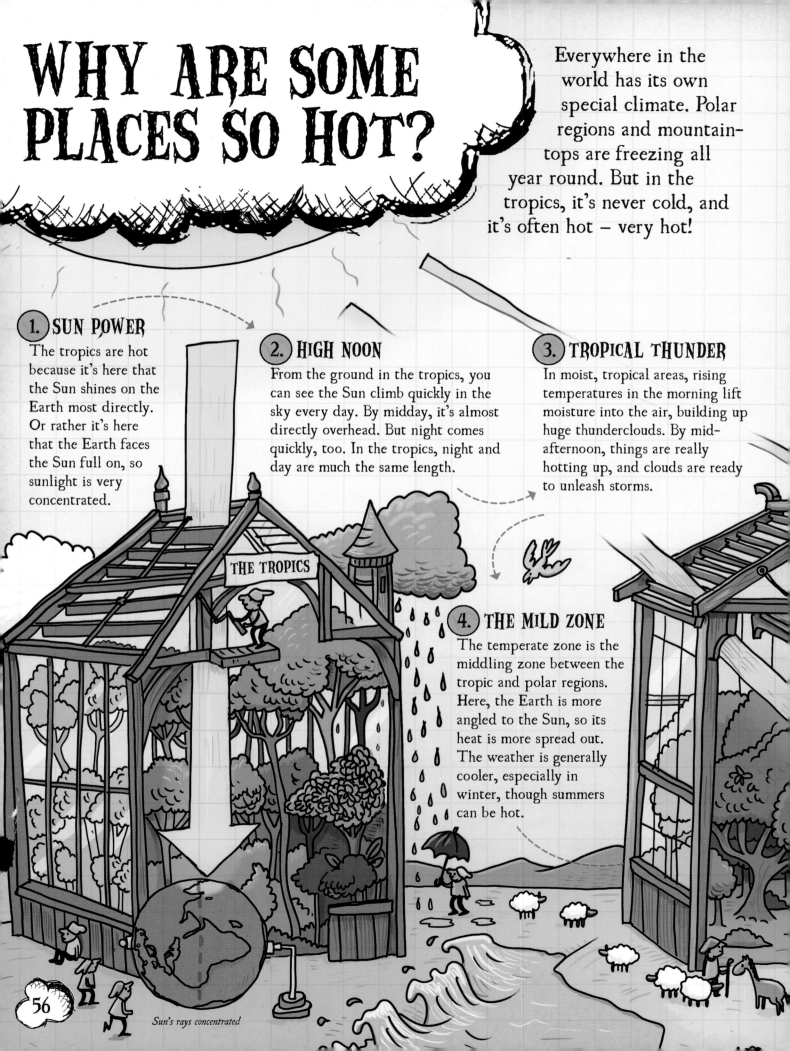

THE TROPICS

56

Sun's rays concentrated

6. HURRICANE'S EYE

Right in the centre, there is a tunnel up through the clouds, called the 'eye'. Here, winds spiral up the cloud walls and out of the top of the storm. When the eye passes over, the sky clears and everything goes calm. But don't be fooled – the lull is brief!

Cold air

Eye

Warm air

Warm air

7. SURGE!

Low air pressure in the hurricane's eye lifts the ocean surface up in a dome. Winds pile up water even higher. This is called a 'storm surge'. As the hurricane moves landwards, it drives the surge with it, creating a massive high tide that can swamp coastal areas and flood far inland.

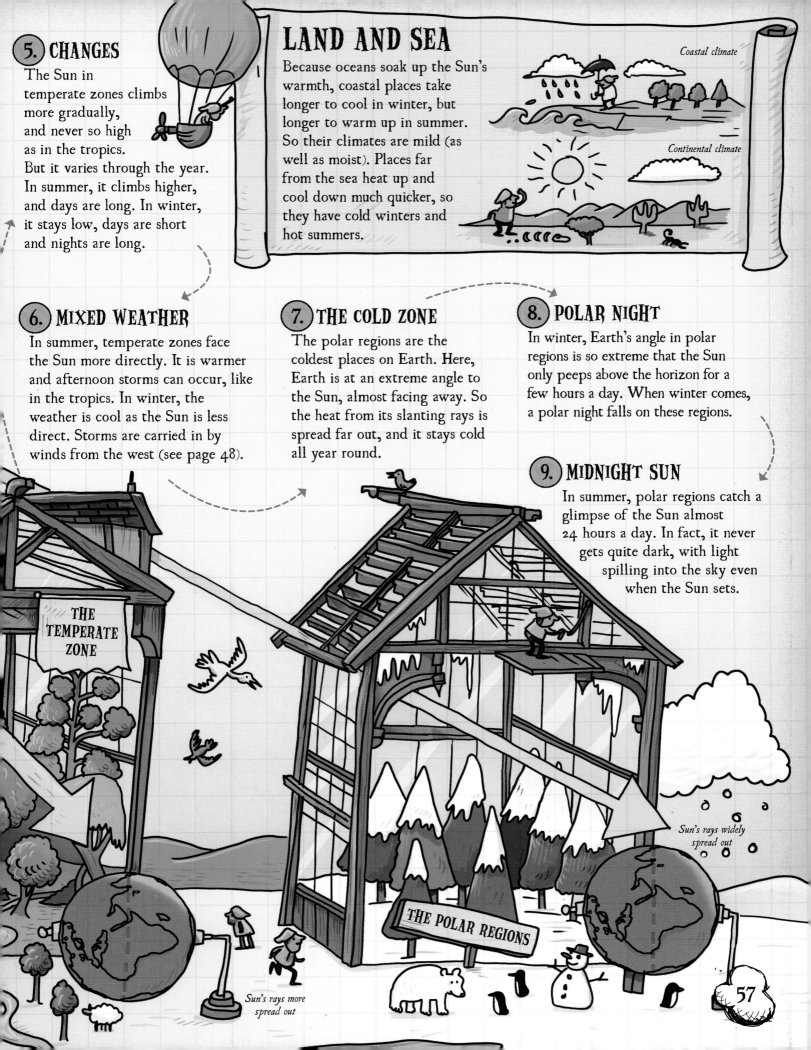

5. CHANGES

The Sun in temperate zones climbs more gradually, and never so high as in the tropics. But it varies through the year. In summer, it climbs higher, and days are long. In winter, it stays low, days are short and nights are long.

LAND AND SEA

Because oceans soak up the Sun's warmth, coastal places take longer to cool in winter, but longer to warm up in summer. So their climates are mild (as well as moist). Places far from the sea heat up and cool down much quicker, so they have cold winters and hot summers.

Coastal climate

Continental climate

6. MIXED WEATHER

In summer, temperate zones face the Sun more directly. It is warmer and afternoon storms can occur, like in the tropics. In winter, the weather is cool as the Sun is less direct. Storms are carried in by winds from the west (see page 48).

7. THE COLD ZONE

The polar regions are the coldest places on Earth. Here, Earth is at an extreme angle to the Sun, almost facing away. So the heat from its slanting rays is spread far out, and it stays cold all year round.

8. POLAR NIGHT

In winter, Earth's angle in polar regions is so extreme that the Sun only peeps above the horizon for a few hours a day. When winter comes, a polar night falls on these regions.

9. MIDNIGHT SUN

In summer, polar regions catch a glimpse of the Sun almost 24 hours a day. In fact, it never gets quite dark, with light spilling into the sky even when the Sun sets.

THE TEMPERATE ZONE

THE POLAR REGIONS

Sun's rays widely spread out

Sun's rays more spread out

57

HOW DO THE SEASONS TURN?

In polar regions, it's freezing cold all year round. In the tropics, it's never cold at all. But in the 'temperate' zone in between, the Earth's journey round the Sun brings the yearly dance of the seasons. Here, chilly winter leads through spring to warm summer then back through autumn to winter once more.

① CHILLY TIMES

In winter, Earth is leaning away from the Sun. The Sun is low in the sky, days are short and the weather cold and stormy. Water often freezes and is hard to come by. So deciduous trees shut down, losing their leaves, and animals may hibernate.

SUN SHIFTS

If Earth was upright, there would be no seasons. But it is on a tilt, so the angle sunlight hits it changes through the year. The point on Earth facing the Sun head on shifts from north to south and back again.

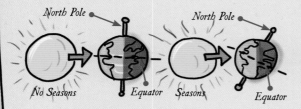

North Pole — No Seasons — Equator — Seasons — North Pole — Equator

THE SEASONAL ROUND

When the northern half leans towards the Sun, the temperatures here start to rise. When it swings round the other side six months later, the north leans away, making it colder. It's the opposite in the south.

21st June — *21st March* — *21st December* — *21st September*

Snow — *Blossom*

WINTER — SPRING

② BLEAK MIDWINTER

The shortest day of the year is the winter solstice. This is the middle of winter and after this, the Earth leans towards the Sun and days get longer again.

③ BLOSSOM TIME

As spring arrives, the Sun climbs higher in the sky and the weather improves. Days are warm, but nights stay cool and it is often showery – perfect for trees to blossom and plants to grow.

8. COLD AHEAD

Day and night gradually even out, until finally on the night of the autumn equinox, they are equal all over the world. The year's two equinoxes are on the 21st March and the 21st September.

7. LEAF FALL

By autumn, the Sun is as low in the sky as in spring. Days may still be warm, but the air is moist, and chilly nights may bring mists. Leaves turn gold and brown as the trees prepare to shed them.

Fruit

Leaves turn brown

SUMMER

AUTUMN

4. EQUAL NIGHT

As spring continues, days grow longer, and by the vernal (spring) equinox, day and night are equally long. On this one day (and the other equinox in autumn), day and night are equal all over the world.

5. SUMMER HIGH

In summer, the Sun climbs high in the sky, so its rays are strong. Days are long and the weather is warm and often dry, with afternoon thunderstorms. Plants are in full bloom and animals are active.

6. MIDSUMMER'S DAY

Through the early summer, the Sun climbs and the days stretch out. The longest day of the year is the summer solstice. After this, the Sun sinks lower, and days shorten into autumn.

59

HOW DO TROPICAL RAINFORESTS WORK?

The rainforests of the tropics, such as this one in Indonesia, are special places for living things, lush and green as a hothouse. Millions of kinds of plants and animals live here. Each one, no matter how big or small, has its own place in the forest and its very own role to play.

1. THE AIRY TOP LAYER

Here and there, the tops of the tallest trees tower right out of the forest into the clear air and sunshine above. These trees are ancient, and made of hard wood – tea trees, ironwoods, teaks. This realm is the Emergent Layer.

2. THE GREEN CANOPY

Beneath the tall treetops, branches and leaves spread wide to catch the sunlight. They create a living roof, a giant umbrella that catches both sun and rain. This realm is called the Canopy.

RAIN WATER

Every afternoon heavy rain pours down on the forest, but the treetops are an umbrella. Long after it stops, rain water trickles and drips down over the leaves.

Swifts

Bat hawk

Serpent eagle

Tree snake

3. HIGH FLIERS

In the treetops, birds of prey watch and wait. Bat hawks swoop on bats and snap up birds such as the flycatchers and swifts, which feed on swarms of flying insects. Serpent eagles hunt tree snakes.

④. MONKEY CHATTER

Orangutans and monkeys sit and chatter on lower branches, or swing off to look for food using their long arms (the orangutans) or tails (the monkeys). You might see a green tree python slithering up the trunk and a clouded leopard crouching in wait.

FOOD SUPPLY

Plant remains rot quickly on the warm, damp forest floor and turn into tree nutrients. The soil is shallow, but tree roots that grow from high up the tree can soak up the nutrients.

⑤. WINDERS AND CLINGERS

In the shade beneath, ferns grow thick and saplings wait for a gap to open above. Strangler plants twist up round trunks to glimpse the sun. 'Epiphytes' cling to trunks and catch rain dripping from above. This area is called the Understory.

⑥. GROUND HOGGERS

It's gloomy, moist and warm on the forest floor. Fallen leaves rot quickly to form a thick carpet, rich with mould and fungi, and little shrubs. This is the Shrub Layer. Plant remains rot quickly on the forest floor and turn into tree nutrients. The soil is shallow, but tree roots soak up the nutrients.

⑦. THE STALKING FLOOR

On the forest floor, tigers, leopards, and dogs called dhole wait to catch oxlike banteng or tiny mouse deer. Moon rats and lizards scurry through the fallen leaves looking for insects.

Orangutan

Monkey

Green tree python

Clouded leopard

Ferns

Moon rat

Tiger

Epiphytes

Clouded leopard

Bracket fungi

Dhole

Banteng

Strangler plants

HOW DO PLANTS USE SUNLIGHT?

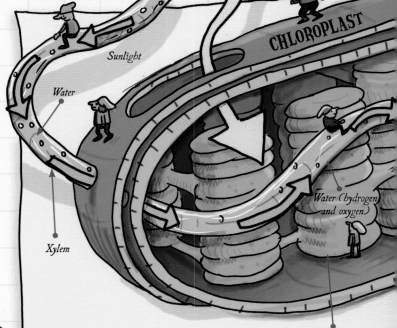

Plants can live off just air, water and sunshine! Green leaves are a plant's food factories, and fuelled by sunlight they transform air and water into food in a process called photosynthesis.

1. PALISADE POWERHOUSE

Leaves are big and flat to catch every glimmer of sunshine. Beneath their waxy topcoat crowds an army of 'palisade' cells, each a tiny powerhouse. Inside every one of them are dozens of amazing green solar cells, called chloroplasts.

Chloroplast

Stomata

Carbon dioxide

Sunlight

Water

Xylem

CHLOROPLAST

Water (hydrogen and oxygen)

Thylakoids

2. WATER DELIVERY

Most plants die quickly without water. Water not only keeps their cells plump and fresh, it's also one of the key ingredients in their food. It's drawn up from the soil through the plant's roots and up to the leaf through pipes called xylem.

3. GAS DELIVERY

Carbon dioxide gas from the air is the second key ingredient. It's drawn in through holes in the bottom of the leaf called stomata. Every stoma has a pair of guard cells that let it in only when needed.

4. LITTLE GREEN GENERATORS

When the Sun comes up each day, the chloroplasts burst into action. Each contains pancake stacks called thylakoids that are the key to it all. They contain a special pigment (coloured substance) called chlorophyll, which is what makes plants green.

5. EXCITED BY THE SUN

When sunlight hits the leaf, it streams into the chloroplasts and pumps the chlorophyll full of energy. The chlorophyll splits water into its two ingredients – hydrogen and oxygen.

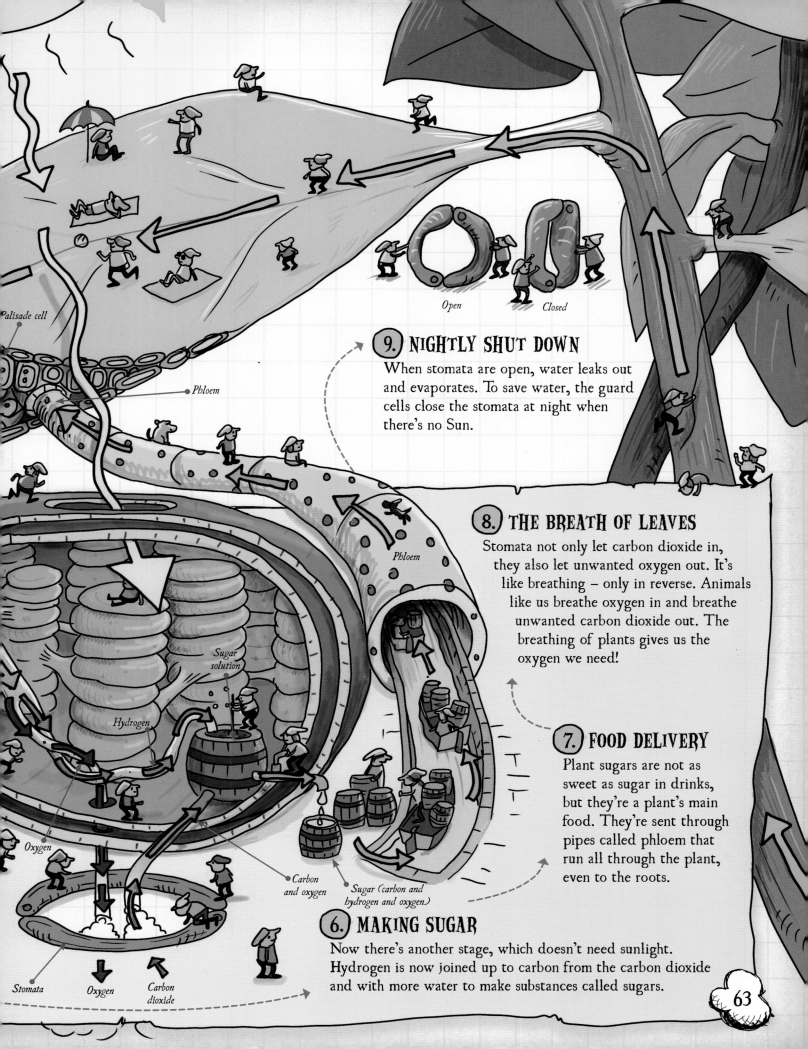

Palisade cell

Phloem

Open **Closed**

9. NIGHTLY SHUT DOWN

When stomata are open, water leaks out and evaporates. To save water, the guard cells close the stomata at night when there's no Sun.

Phloem

8. THE BREATH OF LEAVES

Stomata not only let carbon dioxide in, they also let unwanted oxygen out. It's like breathing – only in reverse. Animals like us breathe oxygen in and breathe unwanted carbon dioxide out. The breathing of plants gives us the oxygen we need!

Sugar solution

Hydrogen

7. FOOD DELIVERY

Plant sugars are not as sweet as sugar in drinks, but they're a plant's main food. They're sent through pipes called phloem that run all through the plant, even to the roots.

Oxygen

Carbon and oxygen

Sugar (carbon and hydrogen and oxygen)

6. MAKING SUGAR

Now there's another stage, which doesn't need sunlight. Hydrogen is now joined up to carbon from the carbon dioxide and with more water to make substances called sugars.

Stomata *Oxygen* *Carbon dioxide*

63

WHAT GOES ON IN THE SOIL?

The soil beneath your feet is not just dirt, but a magic kingdom of tiny creatures, plants and microbes. This teeming world supports the crops and animals that provide all our food.

MUD AND GOO

Making soil begins when rocks are broken down into muddy sand and clay. But rock grains only become soil when life moves in and the grains mix with rotting remains of plants and animals – which in time become a dark goo called humus.

SOIL LAYERS

Tiny pores between the grains fill with air and water and become home to bacteria, algae and fungi. It takes 10,000 years to make soil. Over time, different levels, called horizons, develop, with the top layer richest in organic matter.

SOIL VILLAGE

Horizon – the thin surface coat of rotting plants

Topsoil (A horizon) – rich in humus and minerals

Subsoil (B horizon) – poor in humus but rich in minerals washed down

SOIL DWELLERS

THE DIRT CROWD

Trillions of organisms live together in the soil, mixing it up to give its rich texture. They include microbes and fungi, as well as burrowing creatures such as ants, termites, worms and rodents, and, of course, plants.

These organisms are linked in a web. They are organised in trophic levels, with organisms in each level feeding on the next level down. It all starts with plants, which create food from air and water, using sunlight by photosynthesis.

1 *Plant shoots and roots, algae and lichen feed using the sun.*

2 *Decomposers, such as bacteria, fungi and nematodes, break down dead plants.*

3 *Shredders and grazers, including bugs, nematodes and earthworms, feed on old plants.*

5 *Top predators, such as rodents, moles and birds, feed on the shredders and grazers.*

4 *Tiny predators, such as mites and centipedes, and big nematodes, such as roundworms, feed on the shredders and grazers.*

MOVING INGREDIENTS

PASSING IT ROUND

As soil organisms feed on each other, they pass on key ingredients of soil life in never-ending cycles. They provide plants with the chemical 'nutrients' needed for growth. Plants only grow well in fertile soils that are rich in nutrients.

Green plants take in carbon dioxide from the air.

Animals eat plants and breathe out carbon dioxide.

Animal dung releases carbon.

Plants return carbon to the air as they are decomposed by bacteria and fungi.

CARBON CYCLE

Plants take carbon from the air during photosynthesis. Some gets returned to the air straight away, some returns as the plants are decomposed (broken down by bacteria and fungi). More carbon is released when animals eat the plants and return it to the air when they breathe out carbon dioxide gas.

NITROGEN CYCLE

Plants need nitrogen. There's lots in the air, but it's in a form plants can't use. In the nitrogen cycle, bacteria and other organisms 'fix' the nitrogen and eventually change it to a form plants can take up from the soil through their roots and use.

Decaying plants release nitrogen to the air.

Rainwater carries nitrogen into the soil.

Roots take up nitrates.

Bacteria fix nitrogen as 'nitrates', which plants can use.

C horizon – weathered rock

ROOT CAUSE

Plant roots are a special place where some bacteria and fungi live in a close and often helpful relationship with the plants. Plants give bacteria and fungi sugars to feed on. In return, bacteria give the roots nitrates and fungi help pipe in nitrogen from decaying leaves with their tentacles or 'hyphae'.

D horizon – bedrock

65

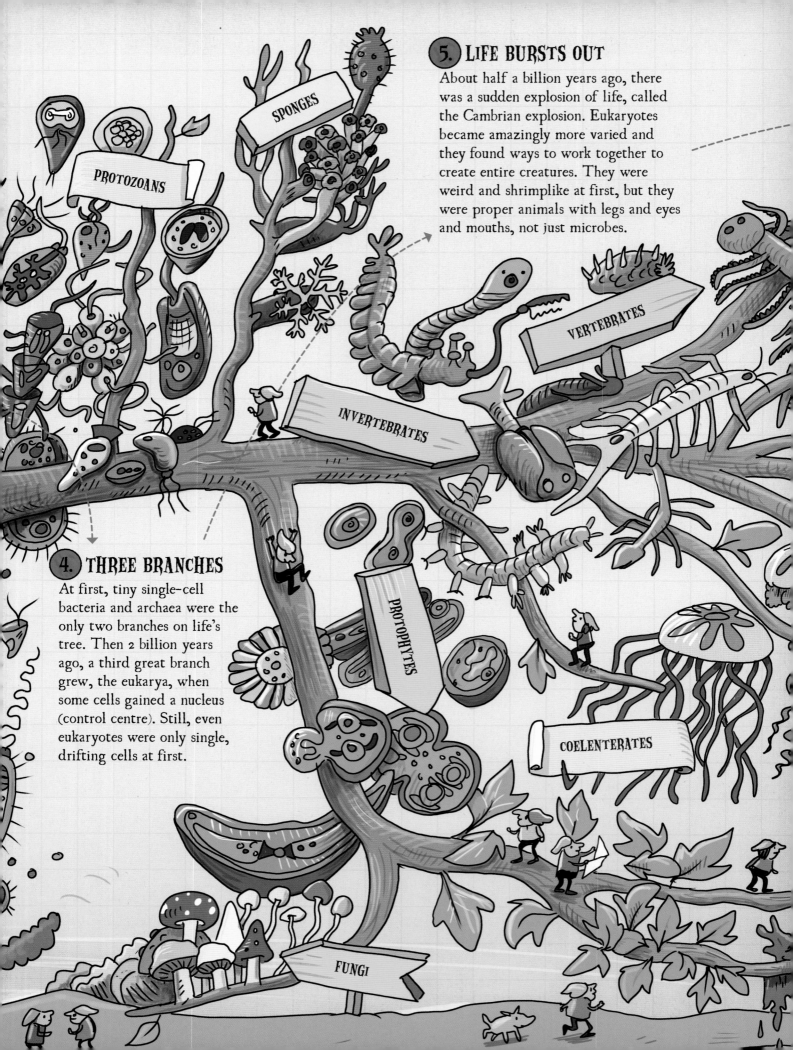

PROTOZOANS

SPONGES

5. LIFE BURSTS OUT

About half a billion years ago, there was a sudden explosion of life, called the Cambrian explosion. Eukaryotes became amazingly more varied and they found ways to work together to create entire creatures. They were weird and shrimplike at first, but they were proper animals with legs and eyes and mouths, not just microbes.

VERTEBRATES

INVERTEBRATES

PROTOPHYTES

4. THREE BRANCHES

At first, tiny single-cell bacteria and archaea were the only two branches on life's tree. Then 2 billion years ago, a third great branch grew, the eukarya, when some cells gained a nucleus (control centre). Still, even eukaryotes were only single, drifting cells at first.

COELENTERATES

FUNGI

WHAT MAKES AN ANIMAL AT HOME?

Every plant and animal in the world has its home or 'habitat'; its own special place where it lives best. Every habitat is home to 'families' of living things that get along together and are well-suited to the conditions.

WARM AND WET

Every habitat has its own special qualities. But the first questions a living thing needs to ask are: is it hot or cold enough, and is it wet or dry enough? So the world is divided into eight great home regions or 'biomes' by warmth and wetness.

TEMPERATE WOODLANDS

In moist, temperate areas, thick woods grow in summer. But when water turns to ice in winter, the trees may lose their leaves. Creatures that live here thrive on the summer plenty, then many hibernate or move away to get through the tough winter.

TEMPERATE GRASSLANDS

In areas too dry for trees to grow, windy, open steppe and prairie grasslands stretch far. Herds of buffalo wander far and wide, over the grass, but rodents and insects burrow into the shelter of the ground under the grass.

TROPICAL FOREST

In the warmest, wettest places, lush, green forests can grow thick. They provide homes for an astonishing variety of animals. More kinds of amphibians, reptiles, mammals, birds and insects live here than anywhere else on Earth. But human loggers are chopping them down.

Colourful parrots and birds of paradise

Hunting wolves

Agile apes and monkeys

Stealthy tigers

66

HOW DID LIFE BEGIN AND EVOLVE?

Beasts, bugs, bacteria and human beings – we're all family. Long ago, the only living things were tiny pockets of chemicals called cells. Then some cells split in half to make new cells. All life has formed the same way since, and so life comes from life.

Cyanobacteria

Purple bacteria

ARCHAEA

EUKARYA

BACTERIA

Luca

3. THE TREE OF LIFE

Through evolution, Luca's offspring branched this way and that like a great tree, with new plants and animals forever emerging. Some are still with us even today. But others lived their time upon the Earth for a while then became extinct (died out).

1. GRAND-DADDY LUCA

About 3.5 billion years ago, there was a tiny cell adrift in the oceans called Luca (which stands for 'Last Universal Common Ancestor'). Luca wasn't the only cell, but was grand-daddy of us all. Luca's offspring have lived through all Earth's ages since, becoming all animals and plants that ever lived!

2. MAKING VARIATIONS

No two living things ever come into the world quite the same. Little differences pop up in each generation. Cells mutate (change) and come together in new shapes. So in time, a sponge can develop into something new. This is called evolution.

PLANTED 3.5 BILLION YEARS AGO

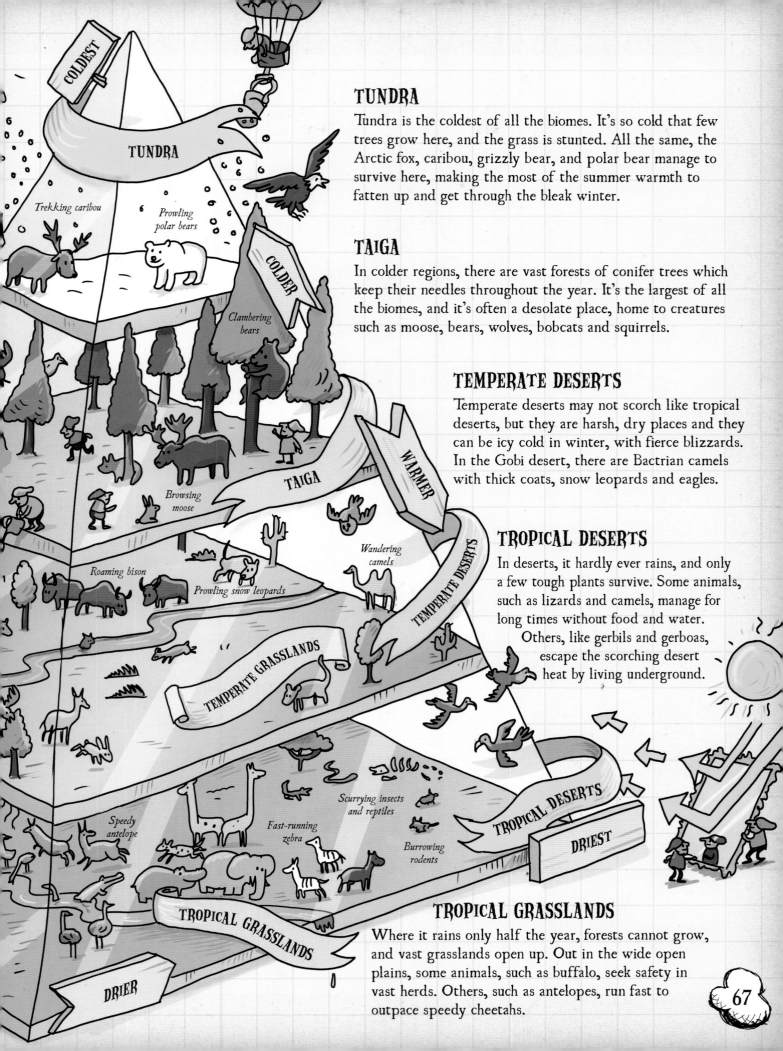

TUNDRA

Tundra is the coldest of all the biomes. It's so cold that few trees grow here, and the grass is stunted. All the same, the Arctic fox, caribou, grizzly bear, and polar bear manage to survive here, making the most of the summer warmth to fatten up and get through the bleak winter.

TAIGA

In colder regions, there are vast forests of conifer trees which keep their needles throughout the year. It's the largest of all the biomes, and it's often a desolate place, home to creatures such as moose, bears, wolves, bobcats and squirrels.

TEMPERATE DESERTS

Temperate deserts may not scorch like tropical deserts, but they are harsh, dry places and they can be icy cold in winter, with fierce blizzards. In the Gobi desert, there are Bactrian camels with thick coats, snow leopards and eagles.

TROPICAL DESERTS

In deserts, it hardly ever rains, and only a few tough plants survive. Some animals, such as lizards and camels, manage for long times without food and water. Others, like gerbils and gerboas, escape the scorching desert heat by living underground.

TROPICAL GRASSLANDS

Where it rains only half the year, forests cannot grow, and vast grasslands open up. Out in the wide open plains, some animals, such as buffalo, seek safety in vast herds. Others, such as antelopes, run fast to outpace speedy cheetahs.

COLDEST

TUNDRA

Trekking caribou

Prowling polar bears

COLDER

Clambering bears

TAIGA

Browsing moose

WARMER

Wandering camels

TEMPERATE DESERTS

Roaming bison

Prowling snow leopards

TEMPERATE GRASSLANDS

Speedy antelope

Fast-running zebra

Scurrying insects and reptiles

Burrowing rodents

TROPICAL DESERTS

DRIEST

TROPICAL GRASSLANDS

DRIER

67

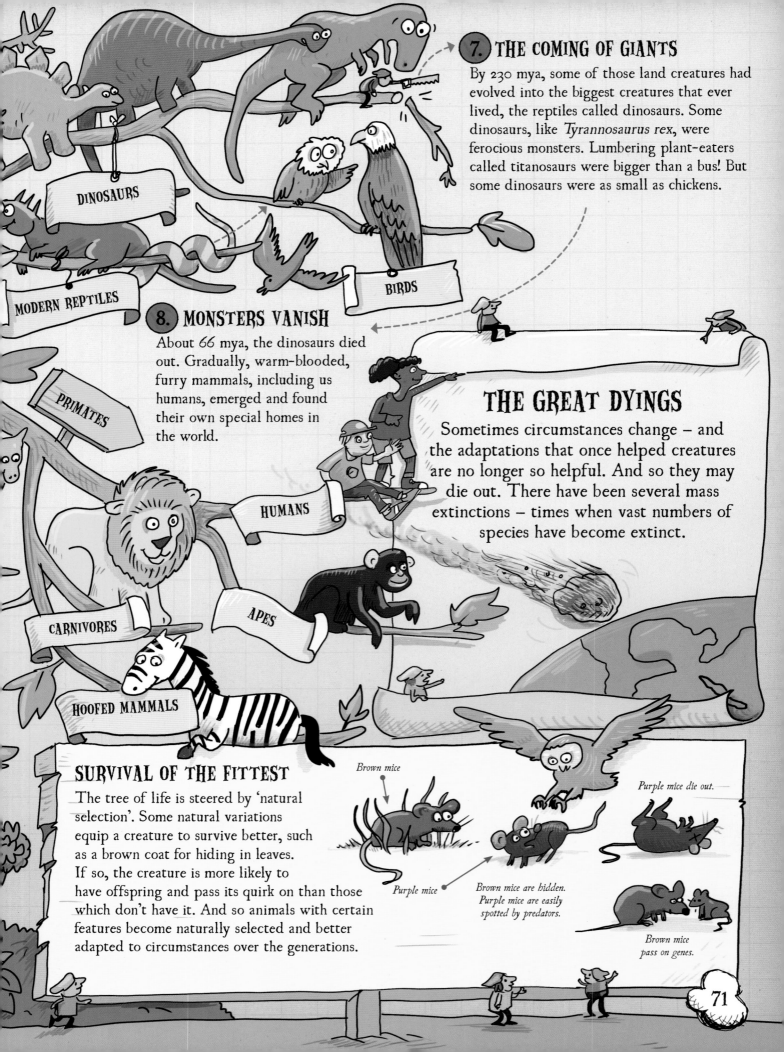

7. THE COMING OF GIANTS

By 230 mya, some of those land creatures had evolved into the biggest creatures that ever lived, the reptiles called dinosaurs. Some dinosaurs, like *Tyrannosaurus rex*, were ferocious monsters. Lumbering plant-eaters called titanosaurs were bigger than a bus! But some dinosaurs were as small as chickens.

DINOSAURS

MODERN REPTILES

BIRDS

8. MONSTERS VANISH

About 66 mya, the dinosaurs died out. Gradually, warm-blooded, furry mammals, including us humans, emerged and found their own special homes in the world.

PRIMATES

THE GREAT DYINGS

Sometimes circumstances change – and the adaptations that once helped creatures are no longer so helpful. And so they may die out. There have been several mass extinctions – times when vast numbers of species have become extinct.

HUMANS

CARNIVORES

APES

HOOFED MAMMALS

SURVIVAL OF THE FITTEST

The tree of life is steered by 'natural selection'. Some natural variations equip a creature to survive better, such as a brown coat for hiding in leaves. If so, the creature is more likely to have offspring and pass its quirk on than those which don't have it. And so animals with certain features become naturally selected and better adapted to circumstances over the generations.

Brown mice

Purple mice

Brown mice are hidden. Purple mice are easily spotted by predators.

Purple mice die out.

Brown mice pass on genes.

71

HOW DO ANIMALS AND PLANTS LIVE TOGETHER?

Around the world, there are billions of amazing living communities where animals and plants and microbes all work together. Some are no bigger than a drop of water. Some are as big as oceans. They are called ecosystems.

1. INPUTS

No ecosystem can survive without a supply of energy and nutrients from outside, their fuel and food. Ecosystem dwellers interact nonstop, and share it all around. It's the sharing of energy and chemicals that binds an ecosystem together.

2. THE POWER OF THE SUN

Energy usually comes from the Sun. As sunlight streams down, it is captured by leaves using photosynthesis (page 62). And as animals eat plants and microbes feed on them, it's shared through the rest of the system.

3. FOOD IS CHEMISTRY

Nutrients come mainly from the air or water trickling through, and no ecosystem can survive long without them. They also come from the non-living parts of the system, such as the minerals in soil.

4. DINING LEVELS

All the animals, plants and microbes eat each other – and are in turn eaten by the others. There's an order in this chain of eating, which scientists call 'trophic levels'. Of course, there aren't really levels like floors in a diner. It's a complex web of interactions going in all directions, called the food web.

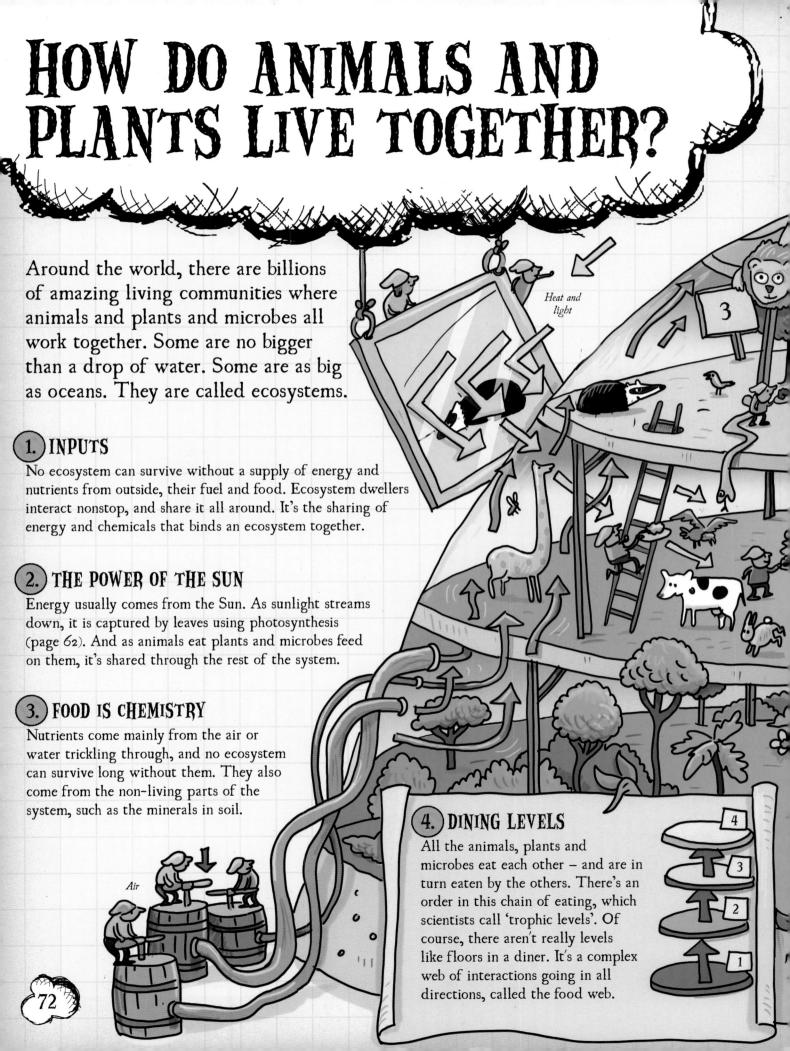

Heat and light

Air

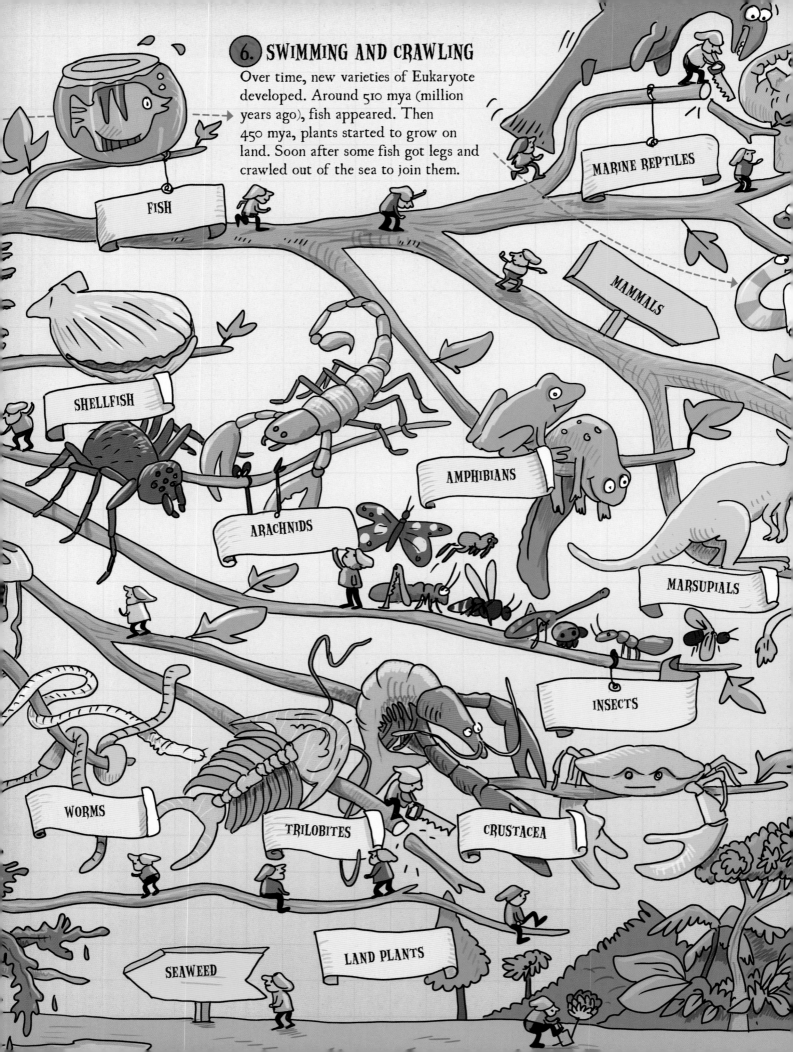

6. SWIMMING AND CRAWLING

Over time, new varieties of Eukaryote developed. Around 510 mya (million years ago), fish appeared. Then 450 mya, plants started to grow on land. Soon after some fish got legs and crawled out of the sea to join them.

FISH

MARINE REPTILES

MAMMALS

SHELLFISH

ARACHNIDS

AMPHIBIANS

MARSUPIALS

INSECTS

WORMS

TRILOBITES

CRUSTACEA

SEAWEED

LAND PLANTS

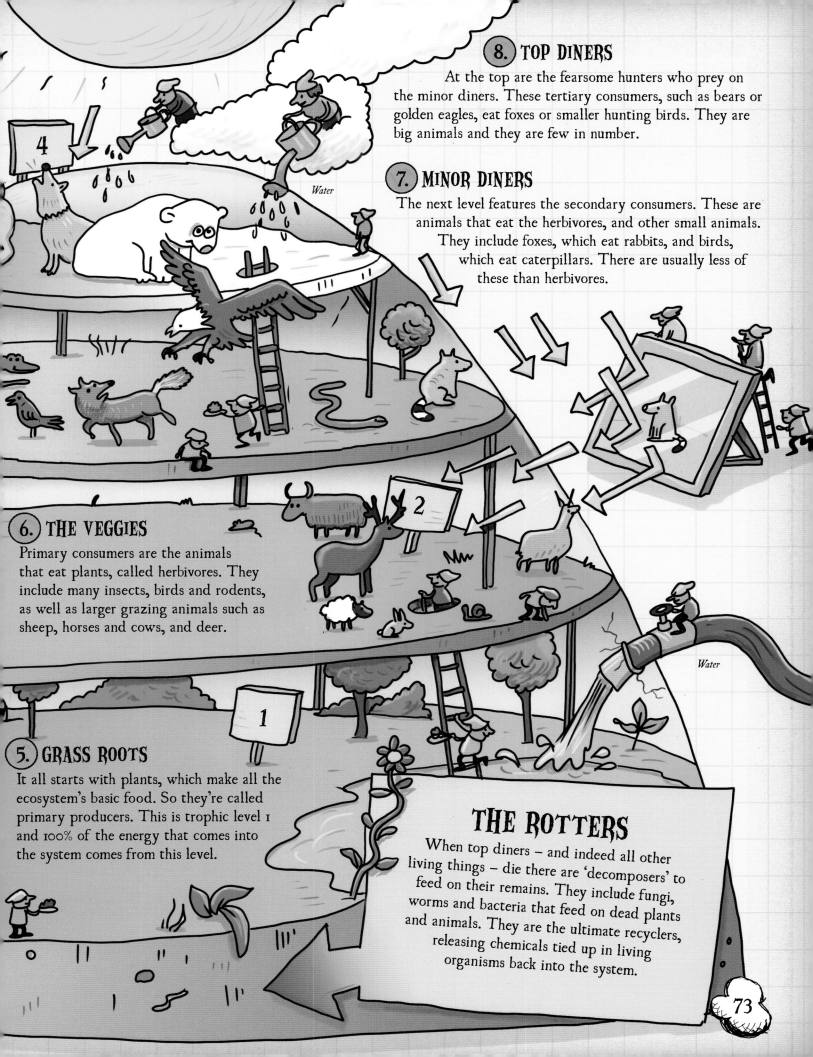

8. TOP DINERS

At the top are the fearsome hunters who prey on the minor diners. These tertiary consumers, such as bears or golden eagles, eat foxes or smaller hunting birds. They are big animals and they are few in number.

7. MINOR DINERS

The next level features the secondary consumers. These are animals that eat the herbivores, and other small animals. They include foxes, which eat rabbits, and birds, which eat caterpillars. There are usually less of these than herbivores.

6. THE VEGGIES

Primary consumers are the animals that eat plants, called herbivores. They include many insects, birds and rodents, as well as larger grazing animals such as sheep, horses and cows, and deer.

5. GRASS ROOTS

It all starts with plants, which make all the ecosystem's basic food. So they're called primary producers. This is trophic level 1 and 100% of the energy that comes into the system comes from this level.

THE ROTTERS

When top diners – and indeed all other living things – die there are 'decomposers' to feed on their remains. They include fungi, worms and bacteria that feed on dead plants and animals. They are the ultimate recyclers, releasing chemicals tied up in living organisms back into the system.

Water

Water

73

WHY DO THINGS LIVE AND DIE?

During its life, every living thing goes through a series of changes. With some flies, it's all over in just a few weeks. With turtles, it can last centuries. These changes are known as life cycles, because whenever an animal or plant has offspring, it all starts over again.

BIRD LIFE

Most larger animals, including birds and mammals, have very simple life cycles. Once born or hatched, they usually just grow in size.

1. Birds begin inside a hard egg. One or both parent birds sit on the eggs to keep them warm until they hatch.

2. When birds hatch, they're called nestlings. The parent stays with them to keep them warm, and brings them food so they can grow.

3. Fledglings are baby birds that can feed themselves but still need parents. In time, their feathers develop enough for them to fly off by themselves.

4. Once adults, some birds fly far off for the winter, while others stay locally.

5. Male and female birds typically begin to court in late winter to early spring.

6. Usually, female birds build a nest for the family. Male wrens build a nest to attract the female.

7. Once the nest is completed, the birds mate and the female lays eggs to begin the life cycle again.

74

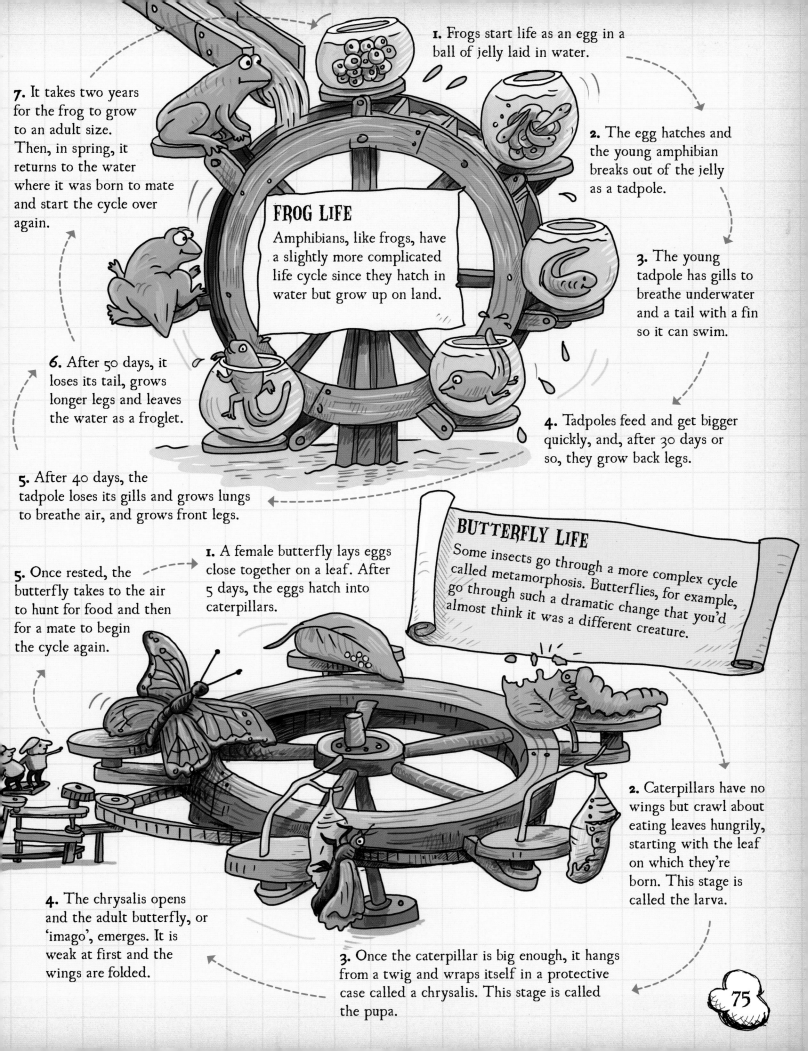

7. It takes two years for the frog to grow to an adult size. Then, in spring, it returns to the water where it was born to mate and start the cycle over again.

1. Frogs start life as an egg in a ball of jelly laid in water.

FROG LIFE
Amphibians, like frogs, have a slightly more complicated life cycle since they hatch in water but grow up on land.

2. The egg hatches and the young amphibian breaks out of the jelly as a tadpole.

3. The young tadpole has gills to breathe underwater and a tail with a fin so it can swim.

6. After 50 days, it loses its tail, grows longer legs and leaves the water as a froglet.

4. Tadpoles feed and get bigger quickly, and, after 30 days or so, they grow back legs.

5. After 40 days, the tadpole loses its gills and grows lungs to breathe air, and grows front legs.

5. Once rested, the butterfly takes to the air to hunt for food and then for a mate to begin the cycle again.

1. A female butterfly lays eggs close together on a leaf. After 5 days, the eggs hatch into caterpillars.

BUTTERFLY LIFE
Some insects go through a more complex cycle called metamorphosis. Butterflies, for example, go through such a dramatic change that you'd almost think it was a different creature.

2. Caterpillars have no wings but crawl about eating leaves hungrily, starting with the leaf on which they're born. This stage is called the larva.

4. The chrysalis opens and the adult butterfly, or 'imago', emerges. It is weak at first and the wings are folded.

3. Once the caterpillar is big enough, it hangs from a twig and wraps itself in a protective case called a chrysalis. This stage is called the pupa.

WHY DOES THE WORLD HEAT AND COOL?

In Ice Ages in the past the world has got very cold naturally, but right now it's getting warmer, and humans seem to be the cause. Warming could give the air so much energy that weather gets extreme, with powerful storms, floods and icy winters, as well as hot summers.

1. GREENHOUSE EFFECT

Air contains carbon dioxide and other gases that work like glass in a greenhouse. They let sunlight in, but prevent its warmth escaping. Humans make the world warmer by adding to these 'greenhouse' gases as they burn coal and oil, and raise cattle.

Infrared

2. SUN

Sunlight pouring into the air is a mix of rays – light rays we can see, along with invisible ultraviolet (UV) and infrared rays. A lot of UV bounces back off the Earth into space. But some is soaked up by Earth and released again as infrared.

Sunlight

3. MIXED

Infrared rays are hot. When a fire glows, it sends out infrared. A lot of the infrared leaks out into space again. But some is blocked by greenhouse gases, and so the infrared warmth is trapped in Earth's atmosphere.

Ice caps

4. WARMER WEATHER

Since the last Ice Age ended about 11,000 years ago, the world has warmed up slowly by about 1°C on average every thousand years. But it has warmed up more than that in just the last hundred years.

5. STORMY WEATHER

The warming of the air changes the world's climate in many ways. It doesn't just make the world warmer – which could turn many places to deserts. It adds energy to the weather, so is likely to make it much stormier, and may even bring colder winters in some places.

THE CULPRITS

Over 30% of all polluting carbon dioxide comes from power stations that burn coal or oil.

Air travel in fuel burning jets is another major source of greenhouse gases.

Heavy industry adds about 13% of greenhouse gas emissions.

Fires burned to keep our homes warm add almost a tenth of greenhouse gases.

Petrol- and diesel-guzzling trucks and cars produce 15% of greenhouse gases.

The farts from billions of intensively farmed livestock release huge amounts of the greenhouse gas methane.

Storms

Greenhouse gases

Infrared

6. MELTING ICE CAPS

The warming makes oceans swell. At the same time, the ice sheets are melting. The combined effect will make the seas rise, putting low-level coasts in danger of flooding.

7. ACID OCEANS

Carbon dioxide also dissolves in the oceans, making them more acid, which can harm sea creatures. This causes coral 'bleaching', and reefs are dwindling.

77

GLOSSARY

Here's a handy guide to some of the tricky words you might find on your journey...

biome A vast natural area with a similar climate and range of wildlife, such as a desert or a tropical forest.

chlorophyll The green pigment (coloured substance) in leaves that helps plants get energy from sunlight by photosynthesis.

chloroplast Green cells in leaves that contain chlorophyll and are the leaves' powerhouses.

cirque Armchair-shaped hollow in the mountains carved out by the head of a glacier.

cold front An invisible boundary in the air where cold air is moving in underneath warm air, creating a line of tall clouds and heavy rain.

consumer An animal that eats other living things.

core The iron centre of the Earth.

core-mantle boundary The dramatic boundary between the Earth's core and its mantle.

crust The thin, solid rock shell of the Earth.

delta A fan-shaped area of land where a river branches out as it nears the sea or emerges from mountains.

earthquake A natural and violent shaking of the ground.

ecosystem A natural community of living things and their surroundings living and working together.

epicentre The point on the surface vertically above the focus of an underground earthquake from which the earthquake radiates.

Equator A line round the Earth midway between the two poles, dividing the Earth in two halves or hemispheres.

equinox When day and night are both 12 hours long all over the world. This happens just once in spring and once in autumn.

evolution The gradual change in living things over the generations which leads to new species emerging.

extrusive The formation of igneous rocks from magma erupting on the surface as lava.

Ferrel cell The large-scale vertical circulation of the atmosphere from north to south and from south to north in the temperate zone.

floodplain A flat plain built up from silt left by a river when it floods.

food web A complex pattern of links between living things that feed on each other.

greenhouse effect The way the Sun's warmth is trapped in the atmosphere by certain gases.

guard cell A cell that opens and closes to shut the stomata on leaves and stop moisture leaking out.

habitat The natural home of an animal.

hypocentre The focus or place where an earthquake starts underground.

igneous rock Rock formed when hot molten magma from underground cools and turns solid.

intrusive Igneous rock that is formed when hot molten magma cools and turns solid underground, without erupting.

joint A flat, vertical crack in sedimentary rock, especially limestone.

larva A young worm-like animal, such as an insect, that will go through a transformation or metamorphosis to become an adult.

lava Magma, hot molten rock, once it erupts on the surface.

lithosphere The rigid outer rock layer of the Earth, forming tectonic plates.

magma Hot molten rock from Earth's interior before it erupts on the surface.

mantle The hot, soft rock interior of the Earth between the crust and the core, almost 3,000 km thick.

metamorphic rock Type of rock that has been transformed by extreme heat or pressure.

metamorphosis A dramatic change in body shape that an animal, such as an insect, goes through when becoming an adult.

moraine Piles of rock and gravel debris left behind by a glacier.

phloem Pipes that carry nutrients in a plant from where they are made to other parts of the plant.

photosynthesis The process by which leaves use the energy of sunlight, water and carbon dioxide to make the sugars they need for food.

producer A living thing, especially a plant, that can make its own food, typically using sunlight.

pupa The stage some insects go through as they change from larva to adult.

pyroclast A fragment of rock blasted apart during a volcanic eruption.

sedimentary Rock made from compressed layers of sediment or matter, such as sand grains, washed down by rivers.

seismic wave Vibration through the ground started by an earthquake.

soil horizon One of the distinctive layers within soils.

solstice One of the two turning points of the year when the day is at its shortest (winter solstice) or longest (summer solstice).

stalactite A needle-shaped mineral deposit hanging down from the ceiling of caves in limestone rock.

stalagmite A needle-shaped mineral deposit projecting up from the floor of caves in limestone rock.

stomata (singular stoma) Tiny opening on the underside of a leaf that lets in gases from the air and lets out water.

storm surge Sudden rise in sea level created by a hurricane.

subduction The process in which one giant tectonic plate is forced down beneath another as they move together.

subtropics Regions of the Earth between the tropics and temperate zone, often with very dry weather.

tectonic plate One of the giant, slowly moving slabs of rock that make up the Earth's lithosphere.

temperate zone A zone between the tropics and polar regions.

transform A zone where two tectonic plates are sliding past each other in opposite directions.

trophic level The position of an animal in the food chain.

tropics The warm regions either side of the Equator through which the overhead Sun moves during the year.

warm front Invisible boundary between warm air and cold, where the warm air rises gently over the cold, creating light cloud and long periods of steady rain.

water cycle The nonstop circulation of water between the Earth and the atmosphere, including evaporation from the sea, rainfall and runoff in rivers.

weathering The gradual breakdown of rocks by the air including the effects of heat and cold, rain and natural chemicals.

xylem A natural pipe in plants that carries water and minerals from the roots to the leaves.

zenith The point in the sky directly above and the highest point reached in the sky by the Sun.

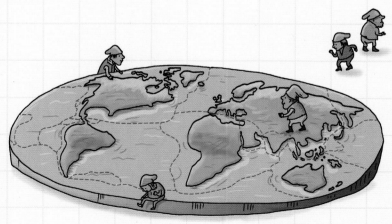

79

INDEX

80